Midlin Times

Midlin Times

Civil War Unsung Hero

Effie Leatherman

Cover & Interior Design by Daniel Horne, Fat Bellied Laughing Buddha, LLC, PO Box 50190, Mesa, AZ 85208.

Copyright 2010 by Effie Leatherman.

All rights reserved. No part of this publication may be reproduced, stored in a retrieval system or transmitted in any form or by any means, electronic, mechanical, photocopying, recording, or otherwise without the prior written permission of the copyright holder, except brief quotations used in a review.

Photograph of Union Soldiers courtesy of National Archives, Washington, DC

ISBN 13: 978-0-615-35409-5

Published by: Leatherman Publishing
PO Box 51449
Mesa, AZ 85208

First printing

Printed in the United States of America.

Acknowledgements

My utmost gratitude and love go to my husband Clete for his patience. He thought this book would never come to an end.

Thanks to my neighbors Mary Obligato and Ann Schubert for their help in clarifying some illegible parts of the diary. An added gratitude to Ann for all the help editing and making sure my comas were in the right place.

We attended the symposium in NC with Professor Michael McCully, and he has kept my computer buzzing. He and his parents, John and Donna McCully, shared the Dwinnell information.

Ed and Sue Curtis from Salisbury, NC, wrote the article on the prison.

Local authors Marilyn Stewart, author of *Footprints & Fragrance in the Outback* and *Child of the Outback* and Daniel Horne, who wrote *Accidental Felons*, shared their experience publishing their books.

Margaret Gardner, wife of Nelson's grandson, Elmer Warren, shared Nelson's keepsakes. Unfortunately Margaret didn't live to see this book because she died last year at 101 in Aberdeen, SD

In the family search I welcomed a newly found cousin, Connie May, who has been searching the family tree for many years. Thanks Connie.

Special thanks for the support and encouragement go to my Apache Junction, AZ writer's group and the time they spent editing this book. Their talent is wide spread.

Our neighbor Larry Welker, for sharing the *New York Tribune* dated April 19, 1865

Finally, Jim Palfini, my computer wizard, who never asked why I was asking the same question over and over, deserves a patience award. He spent hours assisting me in putting everything in order and on CD's.

Contents

Introduction

Chapter I
    Ghosts of the Civil War
    Nelson's call to fight for his country
    Volunteer enlistment
    Discharge
    Nelson's Army Relocations
    Service record of Nelson Slater Gardner

Chapter II
    Roster of Co. A, 19th Regiment, WI Infantry Volunteers *(published by C. A. Danforth, Longbranch, WA)*
    Regimental History
    Individual Photographs of 19th Regiment, Company A *(courtesy of Margaret Gardner, Aberdeen, SD, deceased)*

Chapter III
    Private Nelson Slater Gardner
    Diary, April 21, 1864 to November 8, 1864
    Diary–November 9, 1864 to Paroled March, 1865
    Prison History—Ed Curtis
    Prison Life—W. O. Pietzsch

Chapter IV

Photograph of Solomon Ashley Dwinnell
Record of Reedsburg, WI in the war
History of Co. A., 19th regiment
19th WI Prisoners-most at Salisbury, NC
New York Tribune, Wednesday, April 19, 1865

Chapter V

Photograph of Nelson Gardner-circa 1905
Unsung Hero-by Effie Leatherman, author
Copy of Aberdeen News, dated September 7, 1907
(Pictures of Nansemond River, VA)
A review of the Heroic Act—Company A, 19th Regiment
Letter by N. J. House

Chapter VI

End of Life-Nelson Slater Gardner
His Civil War Mementos
Genealogy
Margaret Craft and the Family Croft Castle
My notes-Effie E. Leatherman, author

Introduction

I carefully closed the leather cover of the weathered diary containing the thoughts of the young man, no more than a boy, who missed years at home with the love of a large family and nurturing parents when he left to fight for the cause.

The Civil War drew men and boys from the fields and factories. They left their families and went into a battle that faced brother against brother, a war that took lives of hundreds of thousands and left many with lasting wounds.

In his diary, Nelson Gardner, my great grandfather, talks of the trials and hardships of his time during the Civil War, especially during his imprisonment at Salisbury, NC

Nelson Gardner adjusted well to his time in the army and yet he maintained his zest for life. His diary states, "*too nite I am titer than a wild owl*". When he went home on leave, he and his buddy "*went out and saw the girls*". He never seemed to miss a good time. Later he wrote of the horrors of the prison camp as well.

I have copied his diary keeping as near to his wording as I could. I knew it was time to share it with all of you. With permission of my friends the McCully's I have added a parcel of a diary from their family. The text shows a higher education and style, but this comrade of Nelson Gardner suffered the same experiences in the Salisbury, NC prison.

The pictures of WI Co. A., 19th Infantry Division are without identification. Hopefully, some readers can supply a name for one that might be from your family.

I could not close the life of Nelson Gardner and these events of the Civil War without listing some genealogy of the Nelson family, his wife and former childhood sweetheart, Margaret Craft. Margaret's family goes back to the Croft Royal family in England, whose family would be another story to tell.

I have included a lot of information between the covers of this book, from the early life of Nelson Slater Gardner, through his struggles of the Civil War to the end of his life. These pages that he painstakingly wrote as a young man gives us not only an insight into his life but into the daily life of the Civil War soldier.

CHAPTER 1

- GHOSTS OF THE CIVIL WAR
- NELSON'S CALL TO FIGHT FOR HIS COUNTRY
- VOLUNTEER ENLISTMENT
- DISCHARGE
- NELSON'S ARMY RELOCATIONS
- SERVICE RECORD OF NELSON SLATER GARDNER

Ghosts Of the Civil War

In researching the Civil War records of my great-grandfather, Nelson Slater Gardner (Gardiner), and reading his diary I was especially interested in the time he spent at the Salisbury, North Carolina prison. This influenced my decision to attend the 7th Annual Salisbury Confederate Prison Symposium held by the United Daughters of the Confederacy — and began a 2,000 mile journey for Cletis, my husband, and me.

We encountered rain, hail and snow and felt as though we were experiencing the old mailman motto: "Neither rain, hail nor sleet will prevent us from our rounds." The spring had brought not only the storms, but the trees and flowers were exploding with color too. Redbud, Dogwood trees, Lilacs, and Wisteria that had climbed to the top of the trees. Magnificent beds of living color lay along and between the highways. Reds, blues, oranges and yellows of all sizes gleamed so many varieties of color that it would have required a pallet of paint in the artist's hand.

When entering North Carolina, we became aware of the reason we were here. The two dozen or more books of the Civil War that I had read became alive as landmarks appeared. We had a feeling of being a part of this history — sensing the ghosts of the presence of men and boys in uniforms of Grey and Blue among the dense trees and foliage.

Salisbury, a town growing in leaps and bounds as all cities across the United States contains an abundance of Civil War history. The Friday evening banquet brought authors of Civil War books. The introduction of the guests revealed that each of those present was an ancestor of a guard, doctor, or prisoner of the Salisbury prison

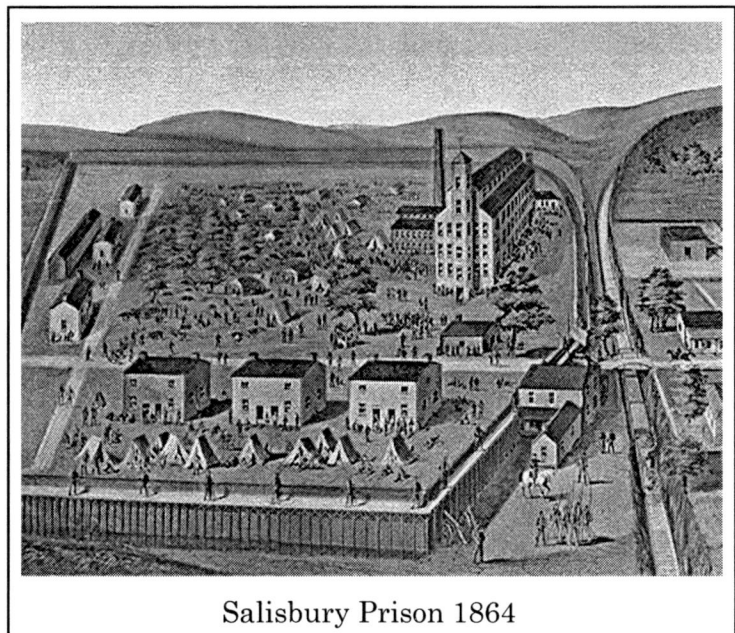

Salisbury Prison 1864

Sunday service in the Salisbury National Cemetery (1861-1865) with a reenactment from the "Blue" brought a sobering time of reflection on the many prisoners who are buried in the marked graves, and the scores of others whose remains lay silent in unmarked trenches.

A similar service was held in the cemetery with the Blue and Grey participating. The Old Lutheran Cemetery dating back to the 1700's is now being honored with markers of those now identified from the unmarked graves at the National Cemetery, GHOSTS OF MANY HUSBANDS AND SONS who did not return home.

Lutheran Cemetery

Our group made a tour of the grounds of the prison site, where houses and a church are now located. Areas where the previous buildings were located were pointed out and the one remaining "Officers Quarters" is now an antique shop.

Agnes, using a cane and with breathing difficulties, walked the area with us. We stopped at her former residence and slowly she sat down on the steps and described the tunnel leading from the basement of the house, the many medicine bottles she had found there,

Midlin Times

and the woman in white with a blue cape that appeared at times during the day and night. "Whenever I didn't feel good she always appeared." Agnes said. "She never spoke, but was just there."

A nurse keeping memories alive of the many that were ill during their imprisonment? Maybe she is still waiting for a release from the ill, those crying out from pain or loss of limb, the weak and the hungry, the agony of war, the lonesomeness for home and family. Will she ever be at peace or will she remain to forever remind us of that time in our history?

NELSON GARDNER had this to say about the prison:

"Wednesday. November 9, 1864, this holy day I am in this prison camp nothing going on here today but it is a hungry tim and mudy and HARD times I should call it if I was a sitison [citizen] but that I am a solger [soldier] I call it MIDLIN TIMES and tho it is the tuffis tim that I ever saw in my lif and I hear will never see a tim again in mi lif but I don't know about it."

"Tuesday, November 15, 1864, too day other boys in my tent and mi self fixt up the tent as warm as we can they ar fore of us and all we have to cover us is a peas of carpit and that bout enuff to cover us but we will hav too make the best of it we can the boys is sitting all the tim."

(the pieces were given to the boys by the town people who cut up the carpets in their homes and churches.)

We left Salisbury with all the ghost and memories of that part of the Civil War and we drove into Virginia. We ventured off the highway near Petersburg and stopped at Five Forks visitor's center.

A monument, cannon, and an "iron horse" in the visitor's center honor that part of the war. At the corner we were drawn to an old barn and a long forgotten log tobacco barn. Just down the road a family cemetery displayed flowers on the graves marking "Mother and Father" surrounded by several white crosses, all this perched in a small grassy area almost surrounded by trees.

Five-Forks Graveyard

We drove on through the pathways of Civil War history until we reached Colonial Heights where we met with my husband's distant cousin, Arlene and her husband Tom. They took us on a tour toward Norfolk and Suffolk, Virginia. There we left the busy freeways and explored the area of the Nansemond River. This river played a significant part in the life of Nelson Gardner.

"On the opposite bank, concealed by tall grass and weeds, the rebels lay concealed and firing with great effect into the ranks of their enemy. Nelson Gardner and a comrade discarded their clothing, placed a supply of matches in their hair, waded into the river. They set fire to the dry weeds on the far bank and the fire spread. Soon the large area of brush that was the hiding place of the Confederates was destroyed. Nelson returned safely to the Union side of the shore, but his comrade was killed while clambering up the bank with him."

My husband and I experienced the sense of the men moving stealthily through the pole-like trees, the heavy underbrush, and the marshes. The enemy lay in all directions around them. Tom was an overwhelming source of information, noting each army movement, the battles won, and those withdrawn.

We stopped at Dabbs house, headquarters of General Lee after the 7-day battle when Lee then took command over General Joe Johnson. Seven Pines was a McClellan supply base on the James River near Richmond.

From THE DIARY OF PRIVATE NELSON GARDNER we read:

> "Friday, October 14, 1864, this morning I took breakfast and had mi likness taken and then got mi transportation and started for Fort Monroe for the frunt"
>
> "Thursday, October 27, 1864, this morning we left our cap[camp] whar we lay for the nit and started in the morning before daylit for the rit of our line and we marched 25

miles and we cam to Fair Oaks what the rebels call 7 Pines and thar we found the rebels in a fort and brest works and our old brigard had orders to tak it and Ole Steng [Strong] hollered out "surrender 19" and while they was taking us we run to the rear and thar we was taken prisoner."

We drove from this area of great battles and were on our way to visit friends at Fayetteville, but first took a side trip to New Bern. Nelson Gardner had reenlisted at New Bern. New Bern was captured early during the Civil War by a large Union army under the command of General Ambrose Burnside and remained under Union control for the duration of the war. Today, New Bern has an impressive historical area, with several buildings still standing.

We continued on to Durham, North Carolina and family there took us for a day to Washington, DC, bringing up in a completed circle of our history not only in the past but what is in the process today. We viewed the Capitol, the Lincoln Memorial, the new World War II monument, and the monuments dedicated to the Civil War. We were in awe of the magnificent part this plays in our unique American history.

Returning to Durham, we completed our journey through the Civil War by visiting the Bennett House where the treaty was signed on Wednesday, April 26, 1865. At the Bennett House near Durham Station, North Carolina, Union General William T. Sherman met with Confederate General Joseph E. Johnson, and final terms of the capitulation for Johnsons' troops were signed. The great war was over.

We began our trip home with memories of the soldiers "BLUE and GREY" not ghosts, but men and boys who gave their lives for their beliefs. Untrained, ill-equipped and without proper medical care, these men fought this Great War.

"FOUR SCORE AND SEVEN YEARS AGO OUR FATHERS BROUGHT FORTH UPON THIS CONTINENT, A NEW NATION, CONCEIVED IN LIBERTY AND DEDICATED TO THE PROPOSITION THAT ALL MEN ARE CREATED EQUAL — THAT WE HERE HIGHLY RESOLVE THAT THESE DEAD SHALL NOT HAVE DIED IN VAIN, THAT THIS NATION UNDER GOD SHALL HAVE A NEW BIRTH OF FREEDOM, AND THAT GOVERNMENT OF THE PEOPLE, BY THE PEOPLE, FOR THE PEOPLE, SHALL NOT PERISH FROM THE EARTH." — Abraham Lincoln

By Effie Leatherman
April 11th to 30th, 2004

Nelson's Call to Fight For His Country

Nelson Slater Gardner came into the large family of John Gardner and Mary Ann Peeso in PA on January 1, 1846. His father had lost his first wife, Polly Abby, the mother of his 11 children then he had married Mary Ann. She had given birth to a son and daughter before Nelson was born, so he fought from the earliest days to keep his place in the large household.

His father had always seemed to struggle to make a living for his family. They lived closely with their good friends, John and Rebecca Craft and their family. They moved to WI to farm the fertile land there.

Nelson was 5'4".with dark hair and grey eyes, slightly built but he could outrun and out shoot his brothers. Whether it was his constant clamoring about joining the war, or his father's patronage, he joined Co. A, WI 19th Infantry Regiment in December 1861 at the age of 15. The call of the war, the excitement of being a part of this great endeavor pulled him from any home attachments. Being an equal to his brothers who had already joined the fight gave him a sense of pride.

He said goodbye to his Father and Mother and those yet at home. The Craft family was as hard to leave as his own family, especially Margaret, who had been a play mate all his life. She was now 13, pretty, brown eyes, golden hair and always with a smile. Her tears were as heart breaking as his Mother's, and he felt a quiver of regret for leaving home.

From the beginning, life in the army suited him. He was adventurous, quick-witted and congenial to all. He states in his diary while in the Salisbury prison, 'it is a hungry time and muddy and hard times I should call it if I was a citizen but that I am a soldier I call it "MIDLIN TIMES." That attitude and fortitude carried him through the many battles and the difficult time as a prisoner.

Note: this is my version-effie

Effie Leatherman

STATE OF *North Carolina*   **TOWN OF** *Newbern*

I, *Nelson Gardner* born in *Stanton Co* in the State of *Penn* aged *Twenty* years, and by occupation a *Farmer* Do HEREBY ACKNOWLEDGE to have volunteered this ____ day of *December* 186_, to serve as a **Soldier** in the **Army of the United States of America**, for the period of **THREE YEARS**, unless sooner discharged by proper authority: Do also agree to accept such bounty, pay, rations, and clothing, as are, or may be, established by law for volunteers. And I, *Nelson Gardner* do solemnly swear, that I will bear true faith and allegiance to the **United States of America**, and that I will serve them honestly and faithfully against all their enemies or opposers whomsoever; and that I will observe and obey the orders of the President of the United States, and the orders of the officers appointed over me, according to the Rules and Articles of War.

Sworn and subscribed to, at *New Bern N.C.* this *27th* day of *December* 186*3*.

I CERTIFY, ON HONOR, That I have carefully examined the above-named Volunteer, agreeably to the General Regulations of the Army, and that, in my opinion, he is free from all bodily defects and mental infirmity, which would in any way disqualify him from performing the duties of a soldier.

EXAMINING SURGEON.

I CERTIFY, ON HONOR, That I have minutely inspected the Volunteer, *Nelson Gardner* previously to his enlistment, and that he was entirely sober when enlisted; that, to the best of my judgment and belief, he is of lawful age; and that, in accepting him as duly qualified to perform the duties of an able-bodied soldier, I have strictly observed the Regulations which govern the recruiting service. This soldier has *dark* eyes, *brown* hair, *light* complexion, is ____ feet ____ inches high.

RECRUITING OFFICER.

Nelson Slater Gardner Enlistment Document

Nelson Slater Gardner Discharge Document

Nelson Army Relocations

12-1881	Enlisted	Reedsburg, WI
12-81 to 1-82	Guard to Rebel prisoners	Norfolk, VA
4/1/1883	While there swam Nansemond River	N-Suffolk, VA
12/17/1883	Reenlisted	Newbern. NC
4/26/1884	Ewins Mill	Fort Monroe, VA
4/27	Boat Frances passed	Cape Hatteras
4/28	Landed	Yorktown
5/4	Boat landed	Fort Monroe, VA
5/5	Landed	Lily Point, VA
6/21	Marched to & saw service at Fair Oaks, VA	Petersburg, VA
8/13	Marched to (close NE of Petersburg)	City Point, VA
8/14	Boat Lory Vanderbilt landed	Fort Monroe, VA
	Boat Fort Washington left	Fort Monroe, VA
	Landed	Norfolk, VA
8/19	Left Norfolk, VA for Haftmar near Camp Randall, WI	
10/3	Left Baraboo for Madison, WI	
10/4	Camp Randall to Madison	
	Chicago-Fort Wayne, Ind.-Harrisburg, PA	

10/8	Cited as straggler-check in for transportation	Petersburg, PA
10/10		Baltimore
10/11		Fort Monroe, VA
10/13	Norfolk to City Point (just above Bermuda)	
10/14	Fort Monroe-Bermuda Hundred	
10/27	Fair Oaks (just above City Point) also called 7 Pines	
	Taken prisoner	
10/28	Libby Prison	Richmond, VA
	Libby to Greensboro, NC, Danville, NC to Salisbury, NC	
2/28/1865	Train to Goldsboro, marched 12 miles	
	Paroled at NE Perry, NC	

Furloughed March 20, 1865 for 30 days

29

| G | 19 | Wis. |

Nelson Gardner
Pvt., Co. A, 19 Reg't Wisconsin Inf.

Appears on

M. and D. Roll of Veteran Volunteers.

of the organization named above. Roll dated

New Berne N.C., Jan 12, 1864.

When enlisted Dec 27, 1863,

When mustered in Dec 27, 1863.

Bounty paid, $ 100; due, $ 100

Company to which assigned A

Remarks: Pvt. Musk'in Co. H & Vol. Musk'd G.C.
19 I Swars of th. from that that Dept.

Book mark:

Sergeant
(341) Copyist.

| G | 19 | Wis. |

Nelson Gardner
Pvt., Co. A, 19 Reg't Wisconsin Infantry.

Appears on

Company Muster Roll

for Jan'y and Feb'y, 1864.

Present or absent

Stoppage, $ 100 for

Due Gov't, $ 100 for

Remarks: Discharged Dec 26/63
by virtue of re-enlistment
as Vet. Vol.

Book mark:

Crosby
(352) Copyist.

December 27, 1863 to January 4, 1864

APR.16. 18290260 1892.

Stop for Transportation $12.48
Returned Prisoner of War
Captured at Fair Oaks, Va,
Oct. 27, 1864. Due him
three months extra pay
under Tel from A.G.O. May
30, 1865.

Record of Extra Pay Received While Prisoner of War

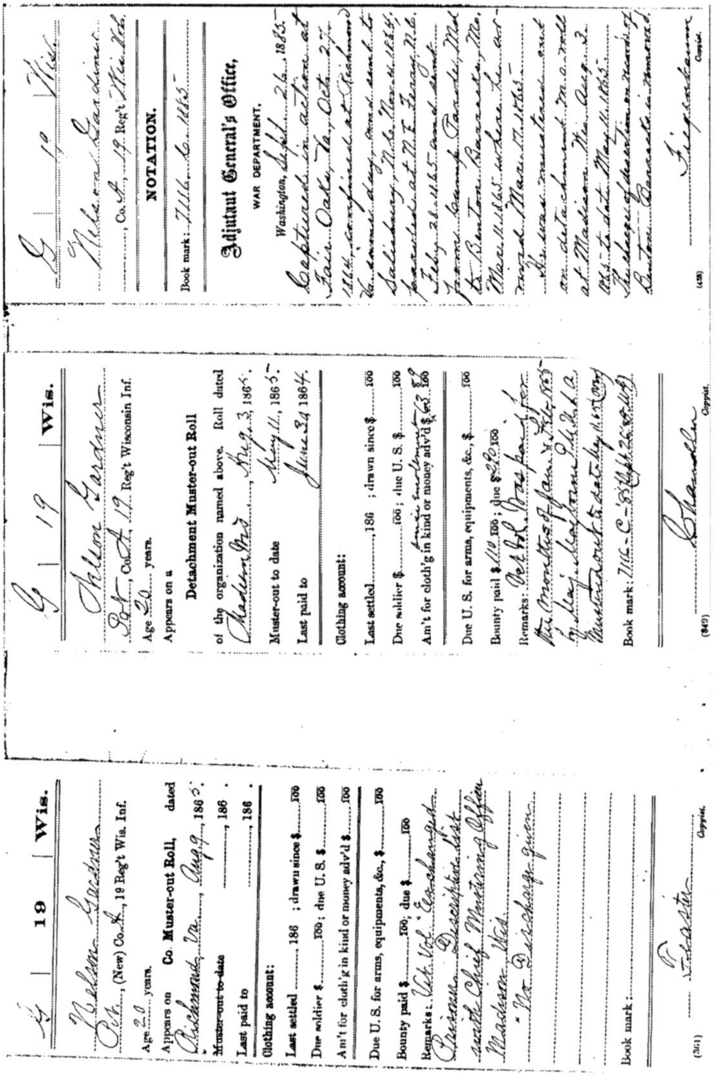

| | 19 | Wis. |

Nelson Gardner

Pvt., Co. A, 19 Reg't Wisconsin Infantry.

Appears on

Company Muster Roll

for *March & April,* 186*5*.

Present or absent... *Absent*

Stoppage, $......... 100 for ....

Due Gov't, $......... 100 for ....

Remarks: *Vet Vol. Exchanged Prisoner not yet returned to Co.*

This organization was consolidated with Cos. A and G to form (New) Co. A, May, 1865.

Book mark: ....

(858) .... *Coust.* Copyist.

| | 19 | Wis. |

Nelson Gardner

Pvt., (New) Co. A, 19 Reg't Wis. Inf.

Appears on

Company Muster Roll

for *May & June,* 186*5*.

Present or absent... *Absent*

Stoppage, $......... 100 for ....

Due Gov't, $......... 100 for ....

Remarks: *Vet Vol. Absent Deserters List with Chief Mustering Officer Madison, Wis.*

This organization was formed by consolidation of Cos. A and G same regiment, May, 1865.

Book mark: ....

(858) .... *Dexter* Copyist.

| G | 19 | Wis. |

Nelson Gardner

Pvt., Co. A, 19 Reg't Wisconsin Infantry.

Appears on

Company Muster Roll

for June 30 to Dec 31, 1864.

Present or absent Absent

Stoppage, $ _____ 100 for _____

Due Gov't, $ _____ 100 for _____

Remarks: Vet Vol Due 3ᵈ & 4th instalments $100. Missing in action near Fair Oaks Va Oct 27/64.

Book mark:

_____ Crosby
                   Copyist.

| G | 19 | Wis. |

Nelson Gardner

Pvt., Co. A, 19 Reg't Wisconsin Infantry.

Appears on

Company Muster Roll

for Jan and Feb, 1865.

Present or absent Absent

Stoppage, $ _____ 100 for _____

Due Gov't, $ _____ 100 for _____

Remarks: Vet Vol Due 3ᵈ & 4th Instᵗ Bounty $100. Missing in action near Fair Oaks Va Oct 27/64.

Book mark:

_____ Crosby
                   Copyist.

(85F)

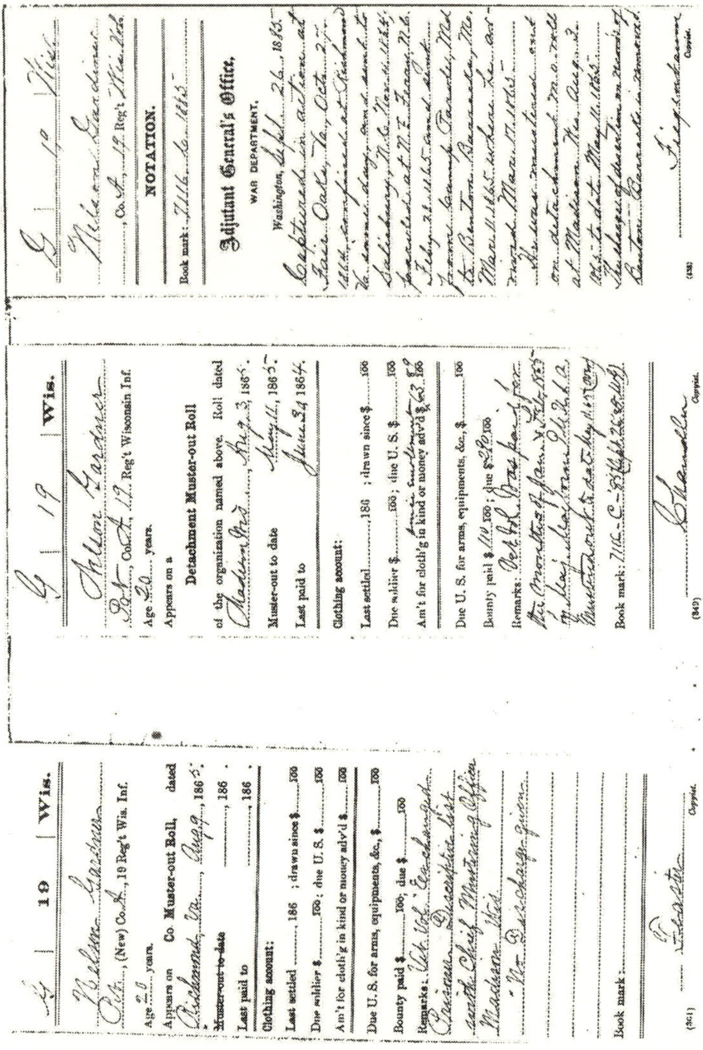

G | 19 | Wis.

Nelson Gardner

Pvt., (New) Co. A, 19 Reg't Wis. Inf.

Age 20 years.

Appears on Co. Muster-out Roll, dated

Richmond, Va., Aug. 9, 1865.

~~Muster-out to date~~ ...., 186 .

Last paid to ...., 186 .

Clothing account:

Last settled ...., 186 ; drawn since $........ 100

Due soldier $........ 100; due U. S. $........ 100

Am't for cloth'g in kind or money adv'd $........ 100

Due U. S. for arms, equipments, &c., $........ 100

Bounty paid $........ 100; due $........ 100

Remarks: Vet. Vol. Exchanged Prisoner. Descriptive list with Chief Mustering Officer Madison Wis.
"No Discharge given"

Book mark: ....

Feaster, Copyist.

(361)

G | 19 | Wis.

Nelson Gardner

Pvt., Co. A, 19 Reg't Wisconsin Inf.

Age 20 years.

Appears on a

Detachment Muster-out Roll

of the organization named above. Roll dated

Madison Wis., Aug. 3, 1865.

Muster-out to date May 11, 1865.

Last paid to June 30 1864.

Clothing account:

Last settled........., 186 ; drawn since $........ 100

Due soldier $........ 100; due U. S. $........ 100

Am't for cloth'g in kind or money adv'd $ 63 89/100 (since enrollment)

Due U. S. for arms, equipments, &c., $........ 100

Bounty paid $110 00/100; due $290 00/100

Remarks: Vet Vol. Was paid for the months of Jan. & Feb. 1865 by Maj. Malcom P.M.U.S.A. Mustered out to date May 11.65 (over)

Book mark: 7116 - C - '85 (Sept. 26 '85 W.H.)

Chandler, Copyist.

(349)

G | 19 | Wis.

Nelson Gardiner

Co. A, 19 Reg't Wis. Vols.

NOTATION.

Book mark: 7116 C 1885

Adjutant General's Office,

WAR DEPARTMENT,

Washington, Sept. 26, 1885.

Captured in action at Fair Oaks, Va., Oct. 27, 1864, confined at Richmond Va. same day, and sent to Salisbury, N.C. Nov. 11, 1864; paroled at N.E. Ferry, N.C. Feby. 28, 1865 and sent from Camp Parole, Md. to Benton Barracks, Mo. Mar. 11, 1865 where he arrived Mar. 17, 1865.
He was mustered out on detachment M.O. roll at Madison Wis. Aug. 3, '65 to date May 11, 1865.
The charge of desertion on records of Benton Barracks is removed.

Fiegenbaum, Copyist.

(438)

MEMORANDUM FROM PRISONER OF WAR RECORDS.

No. 699

(This blank to be used only in the arrangement of said records.)

NAME.	RANK.	ORGANIZATION. No. of Reg't.	State.	Arm of Service.	Co.	INFORMATION OBTAINED FROM— Records of C.Y.B.	Vol. 24	Page. 73	Vol.	Page.
~~Gardner Nelson~~						R. Ex	10	128		
~~Gardner Nelson~~				—		Mis	39	117½	32	47
" " N						C.P. Md	4	394	5	132
Gardiner, Nelson	Pvt	19	Wis	I	A	B.B. Mo	2	135	3	113

"in action" Captured at Fair Oaks Va Oct 27, 1864, confined at Richmond, Va., Oct 27 (Parol from field 15/44 144/11 7/4 87), 1864.

Sent to Salisbury N.C. Nov 4/64.

Admitted to Hospital at

where he died , 186 , of

Paroled at N.E. Ferry N.C. Feb 28, 1865; reported at Camp Parole, Md. date not given 186

Sent to B.B. Mo March 11/65. Where he rept Mch 17/65. Deserted June 20/65.

C/o Mch 10/65. 7116-d-85

Copied by Wer

281

CHAPTER 2

- Roster of Company A, 19th Regiment, Wisconsin Infantry Volunteers

- Regimental History

- Individual Photographs of Wisconsin 19th Regiment, Company A

Roster of Company A, 19th Regiment, Wisconsin Infantry Volunteers

(The Roster was compiled by Danforth in January 1926 and credits are given after the listings of the men.)

Enlistments of these men were for three years and they were mustered into serving the United States Union Army on February 22 through April 29, 1862 in Racine, Wisconsin.

1. Captain Rollin M. Strong. Promoted to Major Oct. 1863 (Sept. 30); to Lieut. Col. Dec. 1863. Commanding Reg't from about May 1864 till Oct. 27. 1864 when he lost his left leg, and was taken prisoner at Fair Oaks, Va. Exchanged Feb. 1865. Discharged March 1865 (April 11). Died Sparta, Wis. 1897. Buried at Reedsburg, Wis.

2. "Lieutenant Henry A. Tator. Prom. Capt. Nov. 1865. Must'd out Apr. 29, 1865. Died on train near Denver, Sept. 24, 1869. Buried at Reedsburg, Wis.

3. 2nd Lt. Alexander P. Ellinwood. Prom. 1st Nov. 1863 (Sept. 30). Capt. May 1865. Must'd out Aug. 9, 1865. Died Reedsburg, Wis. Feb. 6, 1900.

4. 1st Sergeant Emory Wyman. 2nd Lt. Feb. 1864. Must'd out Feb. 22, 1865. Residence North Freedom, Wis.

5. 2nd Sgt. Charles A. Chandler. Veteran. 1st Sgt. March 1864. 2nd Lt. Feb. 22, 1865. Must'd out Aug. 9, 1865. Died San Jose, Cal. July 4, 1902.

6. 3rd Sgt. George Waltenberger. Disc. Jan. 1863 (Nov. 16, 1863, disability). Died at Baltimore, Md. soon after war closed.

7. 4th Sgt. Robert T. Warner. Must'd out April 29, 1865 (1864). Res. Everett, Wash. Died March 28, 1924, Everett.

8. 5th Sgt. Hamer Sutcliffe. Prom. 1st Lt. 1st Loyal Virginians Jan. 1863. (Mustered out Nov. 3, 1864) Res. Portland, Oregon. Died Portland, Ore. 1914.

9. Corporal Martin Seeley. Disch. March 1863 (April 6, 1863, disability). Died Reedsburg, Wis.

10. Corp. Ezra Burton. Vet. Prom. Sgt. May 1864. Must'd out Aug. 9, 1865. Died in Texas about 1907.

11. Corp. Eugene A. Dwinnell. Vet. Sgt. 1863. Wounded Fair Oaks, Va. Oct. 27, 1864. Disch. Feb. 13, 1865, (disability). Res. No. Freedom, Wis. Died Baraboo, Wis. May 7. 1901.

12. Corp. Russell Redfield. Deserted May 1862. Returned Feb. 1864. Private. Must'd out April 29, 1865. Died Warsaw, Minn. 1908.

13. Corp. Alvah Rathbun. Vet. Wd. Fair Oaks Oct. 27, 1864. Died of wound (Hampton hospital) Nov. 2 (5), 1864.

14. Corp. John Faller (Fuller). Vet. Taken prisoner Fair Oaks Oct. 27, 1864. Paroled Feb. 1865. (Mustered out May 17, 1865) Died No. Freedom, Wis, May 12, 1881.

15. Corp. George B. Gibbon. Disch. Aug. 1862 (July 31, disability). Died Baraboo, Wis. Oct. 28, 1913.

16. Corp. Alfred P. Steese. Vet. Sgt. July 1863. Died June 1864 (July 20, disease) at Fort Schuyler, N. Y. Harbor (Hampton, VA).

Midlin Times

17. Drum Major Amos G. Johnson. Disch. Aug. 1862. Dead. (Albert G. discharged Nov. 3, 1862, by order.)

18. Fifer Henry Dwight Root. Des. May 5, 1862. Died Walla Walla, Wash. 1912.

19. Drummer Frank Pettyes. Vet. Must'd out Aug. 9, 1865. Res. Camp Douglass, Wis. Died Reedsburg, Wis. Aug. 15, 1918.

20. Wagoner Rufus C. Cole. Must'd out April 29, 1865. Died Redwood Falls, Minn., June 14, 1914.

21. Ackerman, Dewitt C. Recruit. Must'd. out Aug. 1865. Dead.

22. Apker, James. Vet. Corp. Dec. 1863. Pris. Fair Oaks. Prld. Feb. 1865. Must'd out Aug. 1865 (May 15). Res. Wonewoc, Wis. Dead.

23. Bingman, Isaac N. Vet. Pris. Fair Oaks Oct. 27, 1864. Prld. Feb. 1865. Must'd out Aug. 1865 (May 30). Res. Mt. Tabor, Wis. Died Oct. 27, 1925, Hillsboro, Wis.

24. Brown, David D. F. Disch. Jan. 7, 1864 (disability). Dead.

25. 25. Brady. Peter. Disch. June 1863 (Jan. 19, 1864, disability). Died Reedsburg, Wis. Jan 16, 1907.

26. Bush. Cassius M. Prom. 1" Lt. Co. C, 42nd Wis. 2nd Lt. July 29, 1864). Res. Mexico D. F., Redondo Beach, Cal. Died April 30, 1923 at Soldiers Home, Southern Cal.

27. Brooks, Albert J. Recruit. (From Co. G to Co. D) Must'd out Aug. 9, 1865. Died Reedsburg, Wis. Jan. 19, 1922.

28. Castle, Julius. Vet. Corp. Nov. 1864. Must'd out Aug. 9, 1865. Res. Dallas, Wis. Dead.

29. Castle, James C. Vet. Must'd out Aug. 9, 1865. Died Reedsburg, Wis. Jan. 31, 1896.

30. Cohoon. Lewis H. Vet. Corp. Feb. 1864. W'd Petersburg, Va. July 16(13), 1864. Sgt.Dec. 1864. (1st Lieut. June 21, 1865) Must'd out Aug. 9, 1865. Died Kissimmee, Fla., 1918.

31. Collins, Hugh M. Disch. 1862 (May 11, 1863. disability). Died Reedsburg, Wis. (Aug. 1867).

32. Cary, John. Disch. 1862. Died Reedsburg, Wis., Feb. 26, 1863 (Portsmouth, VA, Feb 19, 1863). (Casey, John. Discharged Feb 12, 1863, disability; died Feb. 24, 1863, Macon Hospital, VA—from Reedsburg).

33. Curtis, James. Vet. Must'd out Aug. 23, 1865. Dead.

34. Cheek, Robert. Vet. Killed in trenches at Petersburg, Va. by a sharpshooter Aug. 7, 1864.

35. 35. Cooper, George W. Vet. Pris. Fair Oaks, Oct. 27, 1864. Prld. Feb. 1865. Must'd out Aug. 1865 (July 31). Died Soldier Home, Minneapolis, Minn.

36. Cole, Dexter C. Died March 7. 1863 at Madison, Wis. ten days after enlistment.

37. Day. Charles. Vet. Des. June 1863. Returned Sept. 1863. W'd Proctor's Creek May 16, 1864, (right leg amp). Died of wd. Hampton Hospital, Va. May 24, 1864 (June 16, 1864).

38. Danforth, Clarence A.. W'd Petersburg, Va. by a sharpshooter Aug. 6, 1864. Must'd out April 29, 1865. Res. Beaver City. Nebr., Tacoma, Wash.

39. Dwinnell, Osgood H. Vet. Pris. Fair Oaks, Oct. 27, 1864. Prld. Feb. 1865. Must'd out Aug. 1865 (June 21). Died at Brandon, Manitoba, Canada, Oct. 17, 1906.

40. Dickson, Albert E. Vet. Des. Dec. 1863. Pris. (New Bern) Prld. and returned Dec. 1864. Must'd out Aug. 1865 (July 23, 1865). Dead,

41. Evers, Christopher. Vet. Must'd out Aug. 9, 1865. Died at Soldiers Home, Milwaukee, Wis.

42. Empser (Emser), Peter. Vet. Pris. Fair Oaks, Oct. 27, 1864. Prld. Feb. 1865. Must'd out Aug. 1865 (June 21). Died Reedsburg, Wis. Jan. 20, 1898.

43. Fosdick, James. Vet. W'd and Pris. Fair Oaks, Oct 27, 1864. Prld. Feb. 1865. Must'd out Aug. 1865 (May II). Died Logansville, Wis.

44. Fosnot, John H. Vet. Corp. July 1862. W'd Drewry's Bluff, Va., May 16, 1864. Sgt. Nov. 1864. Must'd out Aug. 9, 1865. Res. Reedsburg, Wis.

45. Fosnot, Joseph C. Recruit. W'd Drewry's Bluff, Va. May 13, 1864. Disch. May 20, 1865 (wounds). Res. Reedsburg, Wis. Died Reedsburg. Wis. June 18, 1925.

46. Fosnot, George W. Ret. Transferred from Co. E 1864. W'd at Drewry's Bluff May 16, 1864. Disch. July 1864. (July 21, 1865) Died Sparta, Wis, Aug. 16, 1920.

47. Fry, Algernon. Recruit. (From Co. E) Must'd out Aug. 9, 1865. Res. Baraboo, Wis.

48. Fry, Ziba. Ret. Must'd out Aug. 1865 (June 23, 1865). Res. Baraboo, Wis. Dead.

49. Feegles, Henry C. Ret. (FromCo.E) W'd Drewry's Bluff May 16, 1864. Trans. To Vet. Reserve Corps March 1865 (April 24). Must'd out Aug. 25, 1865. Res. Wonewoc, Wis. Died at Madison, Wis. about 1884.

50. Fowler, Henry D. Recruit. (From Co. E) Must'd out Aug. 9, 1865. Res. Elroy, Wis. Dead.

51. Ford, Lorenzo D. Must'd out. (March 30, 1864, disability). Dead.

52. Graft, Giles. Disch. May 27, 1862 (disability). Dead.

53. Greenslit, Martin C. Disch. May 1862 (June 25, 1862, disability). Dead.

54. Grote, Henry. Vet. W'd Fair Oaks, Va., Oct 27, 1864. Must'd out Aug 9, 1865. Died Reedsburg, Wis. Jan. 1916.

55. Gardner, Nelson G. Vet. Pris. Fair Oaks, Oct 27, 1864. Prld. Feb. 1865. Must'd out Aug. 1865 (May 11). Died Aberdeen, So. Dakota, July 24, 1908.

56. Godfrey, Albert. Rct. Trans, from Co. E, June 1863. (Trans, to 2nd U. S. Vols., March 1, 1865.) Must'd out Aug. 1865. Dead.

57. Gerrigan, (Garrigan) Patrick. Vet. W'd Drewry's Bluff May 1864. Pris. Fair Oaks, Oct. 27, 1864. Prld. Feb. 1865. Must'd out Aug. 1865 (June 21). Died at O'Neal, Nebr.

58. Hobby, James M. Vet. Pris. Fair Oaks, Oct. 27, 1864. Prld. Feb. 1865. Must'd out Aug. 1865 (June 30). Died in Boston, Mass, many years ago.

59. Hobby, William D. Died in hospital at Norfolk, Va., Aug. 1863 (Yorktown, VA, disease, July 31, 1863).

60. Hunter, George S. Discharged (March 12) 1863 (disability). Dead.

61. Harris, Edward. Disch. 1863 (Nov. 24, 1862, disability). Died Chetek, Wis.

62. Hudson, John L. Trans, to Vet. Res. Corp(Sept. 2, 1863). Must'd out (April 29, 1865). Died Logansville, Wis.

63. Hurly, Timothy. Deserted. March 1862.

64. Hollingshead, John L. Vet. Pris. Fair Oaks. Prld. Feb. 1865. Des. to enemy Jan. 1865, and returned to Co., Must'd out Aug. 9, 1865. Dead.

65. Haines, Ephraim. Vet. W'd Petersburg July 5, 1864. Died of wound about July 10, 1864 in hospital at Portsmouth, Va.

66. Horsch, William. Died in hospital, 1864 (Hampton, VA, disease, July 29, 1864).

67. Holt, Charles. Vet. Must'd out Aug. 9, 1865. Dead.

68. Holton, William W. Ret. W'd Petersburg, Va. July 5, 1864. Must'd out Aug. 9, 1865. Died Reedsburg, Wis. June 9, 1893.

69. Holton, Thomas J. Recruit, Must'd out Aug. 9, 1865. Died Reedsburg, Wis. Dec. 13, 1922.

70. Hoefer (Hoefle), Michael. Vet. Must'd out Aug. 9, 1865. Dead.

71. Howard, Sidney A. Vet. Must'd out Aug. 9, 1865. Dead.

72. Howard, Harry (Harvey) G. Recruit Must'd out Aug. 9, 1865. Dead.

73. Hopkins, Newton James Ret. Must'd out Aug. 1865 (disability). Died at Baraboo, Wis. March 31, 1910.

74. Harbel, (Herbel) Jacob. Vet. Must'd out Aug. 9, 1865. Dead.

75. Harseim (Harsum), William. Ret. Must'd out Aug. 9, 1865. Died Atkin, Minn. April 28, 1904.

76. Johnson, Thomas J. Trans, to Co. E June 1, 1863. (Pris. Oct. 27. 1864). (Must'd out June 23, 1865). Dead.

77. Kyle, Henry H. (Pris. Oct 27, 1864 Fair oaks). Must'd out April 29, 1865. Died Sparta, Wis. Sept. 1, 1924.

78. Kivell, Michael. Disch. Nov. 6, 1862 (disability). Died Winfield, Wis. March 27, 1872(7). 103 years old.

79. Kipp, Benjamin S. Recruit. Must'd out Aug. 9, 1865. Res. Dallas, Wis. Died Barron, Wis. Sept. 25, 1924.

80. Kennedy, Chauncy. Substitute. Must'd out Aug. 9, 1865. Died Sparta, Wis. Sept. 10, 1887.

81. Kennedy, Clark H. Vet. Must'd out Aug. 9, 1865. Dead.

82. Kennedy, Benjamin. Recruit. Must'd out Aug. 1865 (May 31, 1865). Died Rhinelander, Wis., Feb. 1924.

83. Livingston, Giles. Vet. Pris. Fair Oaks, Oct. 27, 1864. Prld. Feb. 1865. Must'd out Aug. 1865 (May 15). Dead.

84. Leonard, Edward. Vet. Must'd out Aug. 9, 1865. Died Minneapolis, Minn., June 18, 1913. Buried Reedsburg, Wis.

85. Lee, Byron B. Recruit. Must'd out Aug. 9. 1865. Died Baraboo, Wis., June 15, 1906.

86. Miller. William. Vet W'd and pris. Fair Oaks, Oct. 27, 1864. Died of wound in Richmond, Va., Oct. 29, 1864 (Nov. 1, 1864).

87. Millard, Eleazer. Vet. Corp. Nov. 1864. Must'd out Aug. 9, 1865. Res. Chetek, Wis. Died June 1918.

88. Mallow, William. Vet. Must'd out Aug. 9, 1865. Dead.

89. Mallow, Jesse M. Vet. W'd Petersburg, Va. June 22, 1864. Corp. Nov. 1864. Must'd out Aug. 9, 1865. Died Minneapolis, Minn.

90. Mallow, Adolphus P. Recruit. Must'd out Aug. 9, 1865. Died Hillsboro, Wis.

91. Mallow, Jesse, Sr. Recruit Died Hampton Hospital. Va.. April 4, 1864.

92. Mead, George. Disch. May 1862 (Sept. 7, 1862, disability). Died Reedsburg, Wis. Feb. 15, 1907.

93. Markee, James. Died in hospital Norfolk, Va., Oct. 2, 1862 (Oct. 12, 1862, disease).

94. Mallon, (Mallow) John. W'd June 22, 1864 in siege of Petersburg. (Prisoner Fair Oaks, Oct. 27, 1864.) Must'd out April 29, 1865. Died Reedsburg, Wis. Jan. 13, 1914.

95. Pitts, Benjamin S. Vet. Corp. Dec. 1863. Killed at Drewry's Bluff, Va. May 16, 1864. (Missing in Action).

96. Pitts, Newman W. Vet. W'd at Proctor's Creek, Va. May 13, 1864. Pris. Fair Oaks, Va., Oct 27, 1864. Died Salisbury, NC Prison, Jan. 16, 1865 (disease).

97. Pitts, William. Ret. Died Hampton Hospital, Va. 1864. (? Mustered out June 23, 1865).

98. Paddock, George J. Vet. Must'd out Aug. 9, 1865. Died Baraboo, Wis. March 18, 1924.

99. Paddock, Edwin B. Ret. Must'd out Aug. 9, 1865. Died at Soldiers Home Hot Springs, So. Dak. Sept. 11, 1913.

100. Pettyes, Amos. Vet. Fifer May 1862. Disch. Feb. 1864 (Feb 22, 1865). Died Endeavor, Marquette County, Wis., July 4, 1880.

101. Palmer, Ferris B. Vet. Sgt. Aug. 1864. Killed Fair Oaks, VA. Oct. 27, 1864.

102. Palmer, Edgar L. Vet. Must'd out Aug. 9, 1865. Res. Baraboo, Wis.

103. Pietzsch (Peitzsch), Walter O. Vet. Pris. Fair Oaks. Prld. Feb. 1865. Must'd out Aug. 1865 (June 23,1865). Res. Madison, Wis. Died Madison, Wis., April 22, 1924.

104. Reynolds, William T. Vet W'd Drewry's Bluff, Va. May 16, 1864. Must'd out Aug. 1865 (Sickness). Dead.

105. Robinson, Henry. Recruit. Must'd out Aug. 9, 1865. Died Soldiers Home, Chicago, Ill.

106. Sheldon, Charles F. Must'd out Aug. 1865 (April 29). Died Reedsburg, Wis., Feb. 27, 1922.

107. Sheldon, Dewelton M. Must'd out April 29, 1865. Died Reedsburg, Wis., 1921.

108. Sheldon, Kirk W. Recruit. Must'd out Aug. 9, 1865. Died Eddyville, Neb.

109. Sheldon, Harlow. Disch. Apr. 1862. Res. Reedsburg, Wis. Dead.

110. Swetland, Seth. Disch. July 21, 1863 (disability). Died Minnesota.

111. Swetland, William. Vet. Corp. Nov. 1864. Sgt. Jan. 1865. (2nd Lt. Aug31, 1865.) Must'd out Aug. 9, 1865. Dead.

112. Swetland, William T. Recruit. (Wounded April 22, 1864.) Must'd out Aug. 9, 1865. Res. Reedsburg, Wis. Died Reedsburg, Dec. 10, 1923.

113. Swetland, Artemus G. Recruit. Must'd out Aug. 1865 (May 19). (Musician). Dead.

114. Sanborn, Daniel, Jr. Vet. W'd and pris. Fair Oaks, Va. Prld. Feb. 1865. Died Feb. 1865 (March 20, 1865) at LaValle, Wis (Annapolis, VA).

115. Sanborn, Reuben. Recruit. Must'd out Aug. 9, 1865. Res. LaValle, Wis. Died LaValle, Wis., Oct. 2, 1924.

116. Street, Samuel. Died in hospital, July 2, 1864 (disease).

117. Street, Henry. Recruit. Must'd out Aug. 9, 1865. Died Tomah, Wis., Dec. 11, 1923.

118. Stowe, Henry E. Disch. 1862 (Feb. 12, 1863, disability). Dead.

119. Stone, Charles H. Disch. Jan. 7, 1864 (disability). Died Reedsburg, Wis. Oct. 16, 1894.

120. Stocks, John H. Recruit. Must'd out Sept. 1865 (June 23). Died Chicago, 111.

121. Steese, William. Disch. 1862 (Feb. 13, 1863, disability). Dead.

122. Searles, Sylvester. Vet. Killed Petersburg, Va. by a sharpshooter June 29, 1864.

123. Stall, James H. Recruit. W'd Drewry's Bluff, Va. May 16, 1864. Disch. Feb. 20, 1865 (wounds). Dead.

124. Seaman, Harmanus V. V. Disch. May 24, 1863 (disability). Dead.

125. Santos, Hiram. Recruit. (From Co. G). Must'd out Aug. 1865 (May 16, 1865). Died Wonewoc, Wis.

126. Sprowl, James. Recruit. Must'd out Aug. 9, 1865. Res. No. Freedom, Wis. Died No. Freedom March 1, 1924.

127. Tuttle, Albert C. Recruit. W'd Drewry's Bluff, Va. May 16, 1864. Disch. Jan 30, 1865. Died Baraboo, Wis. Dec. 6, 1903.

128. Thorn, John. W'd Drewry's Bluff, Va. May 16, 1864. Must'd out April 29, 1865. Died New London, Wis. Feb. 1888.

129. Thorn. Richard. Vet. W'd Fair Oaks, Va, Oct. 27, 1864. Must'd out Aug. 9, 1865. Died Sugarbush, Wis. Feb. 12, 1925.

130. Townsend, Richard C. Disch. May 1863 (June 17, 1863, disability). Dead.

131. Tillotson, Oliver E. Trans, to Vet. Reserve Corps 1863 (Feb. 15. 1864). Died St. Clair, Minn.

132. Taylor, James A. Disc. 1862. Died Soldiers Home Port Orchard, Wash. 1918. (Musician).

133. Wheeler, Edson. Corp. Aug. 1862. Must'd out Feb. 22 (25), 1865. Dead.

134. Weidman, Alexander. Disch. Jan. 1864 (Feb. 4, disability). Died Reedsburg, Wis. Oct. 1905.

135. Winnie, Menzo. Disch. Jan. 21, 1864 (disability). Died Reedsburg, Wis. Feb. 14, 1892.

136. Ward, Orson S. Disch. May 1862 (July 24, disability). Dead.

137. Waldron, Henry E.. Deserted May 30, 1862.

138. Werron, John. Vet. Must'd out Aug. 9. 1865. Died No. Freedom, Wis. Oct. 26, 1893.

139. Winchester, Franklin S. Vet. Pris. Fair Oaks, Va, Oct. 27, 1864. Prld. Feb. 1865. Must'd out Aug. 1865 (May 13). Res. Reedsburg, Wis. Died Baraboo, Wis., 1916.

140. Wisner, James. Recruit. (From Co. E) Must'd out Aug. 9, 1865. Died Baraboo, Wis.

141. Lamphier (Lamphear), Samuel (Silas A.). Transferred from Co. G. Must'd out Aug. 9, 1865.

142. Sewell, Samuel. Transferred from Co. G. Must'd out Aug. 1865.

143. Sheridan, James. Transferred from Co. G. Must'd out Aug. 1865 (June 11, 1865).

144. Shankland (Shanklin). James. Transferred from Co. G. Must'd out Aug. 9, 1865.

145. Smith, James. Transferred from Co. K. (Sergt.) Must'd out Aug. 1865. (Prisoner Fair Oaks, Oct. 27. 1864). (Died June 14, 1865, Sheboygan, WI).

146. Smith, Frank. Transferred from Co. K. Must'd out Aug. 1865.

147. Rathbun, Ernest (Everett) C. Transferred from Co. K. Must'd out Aug. 1865 (June 23).

148. Richards, John. Transferred from Co. K. Must'd out Aug. 1865

Regimental History

(The items in parentheses in this "Roster of Company A, 19th Regiment, Wisconsin" are comparative information from: Roster of Wisconsin Volunteers. Vol. 2. compiled by J. M. Rusk & C. P. Chapman, 1886, pages 112-139.)

After organization, muster in, and some drill, the Nineteenth was ordered to Madison Wis. on the 25th of April to guard Confederate prisoners. That was easy. May 30, Co.s A and B with all the prisoners were sent to Camp Douglass, Chicago. In a few days the other eight Co.s came on and the entire regt. went on to Washington D. C. From there to Fort Monroe by boat, and then out to Old Hampton where we drilled some more. June 18 were sent to Yorktown, and in a few days back to Hampton. June 27 to Norfolk and the Nineteenth was the main regt, guarding the city with its large stores of Quarter Master goods for the army and the navy. Co. A was stationed on Ferry Point. Ten happy months in Norfolk, barring a little ague now and then. April 15 we were in the siege (?) of Suffolk by Gen. Longstreet. More ague, and more fever. June 16 back to Yorktown again. In a few days to West Point, Va. and in July back to Yorktown again. In Aug. there were not enough well men in the regt. to take care of the sick. On this report we were sent to Newport News for our health. This was Aug. 10. Newport News was absolutely nothing then but a name, and a fine sandy beach for bathing. But it was a healthy place, and about the only one we found in all the "Old Virginny lowlands low." Oct. 9 we started for New Bern N. C. Oct. 14, Co. A was detailed to guard Evan's MJH, an outpost 8 miles south of New Bern. In the six months we were there, the Johnnies attacked us but once, but the ague was with us all the time. April 28, 1864 we were in Yorktown again, assigned to the 3rd Brigade, 1^s'Div., 18th A. C. and May 4 were at Bermuda Hundred with the 10th A. C., all under Gen. Butler. Co. A lost quite a number of men on the Ft Darling expedition. Proctor's Creek, and Drewry's Bluff, from May 13 to May 16. June 15 and 16 the Army of the Potomac began to join us, and the preliminary battles in front of Petersburg were fought on those days. After that, the 9 months siege. Often, too often, one of Co. A was killed or wounded in the trenches. I got mine from a sharpshooter Aug. 6, 1864, and never saw the Regt. afterward. The greatest loss to Co. A was at the 2nd battle of Fair Oaks Oct. 27, 1864, when nearly all the Regt. present were killed, wounded or captured. Lt. Col. Strong, commanding, was captured and lost a leg.

The Non-veterans were mustered out April 29, 1865. The Veterans (those who re-enlisted for the war) and the recruits in Aug. 1865.

The silent figures of the Roster tell a tale not written in the histories. The story of the company, their sacrifices, losses in young lives and shortened years of many more, are all told after their names in this Roster. This Volunteer Co., perhaps the average, was one of many thousands of that army which carried the Union Cause through to victory in the four years of Civil War. The people of this nation have treated us well, given us much honor, but we have deserved it, as this Roster shows. And now, who will say, that the peace, happiness, prosperity, power and influence, of the people of this greatest of all nations is not largely due to the efforts of this Grand Army during, and since the Civil War.

Longbranch, Wash.   C. A. Danforth

January 1926

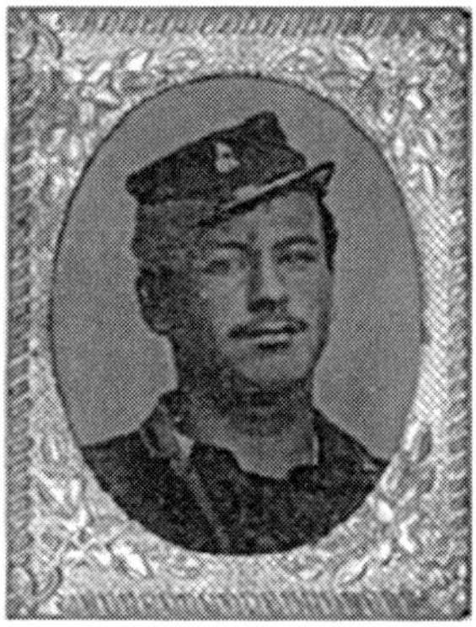

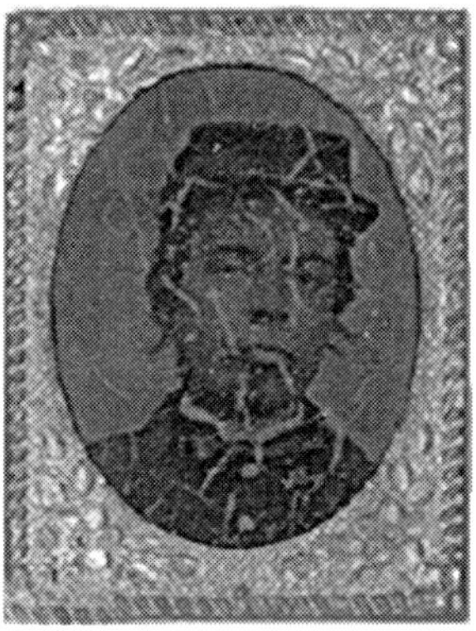

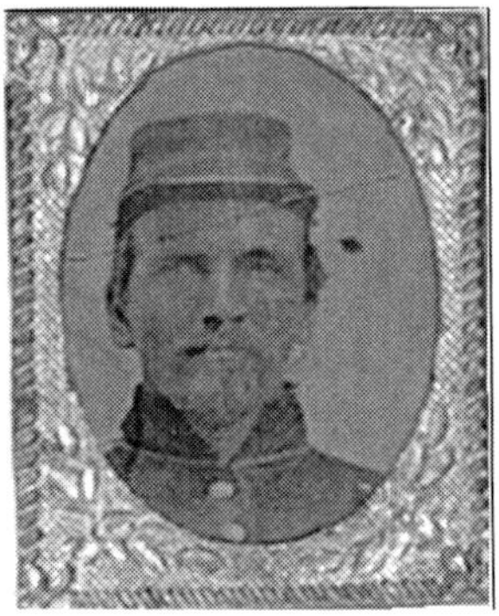

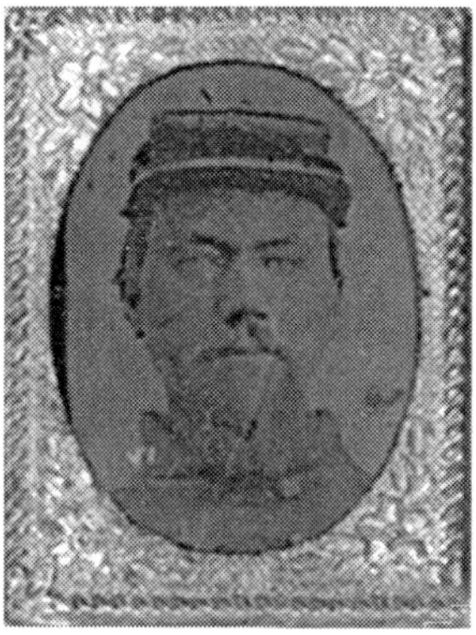

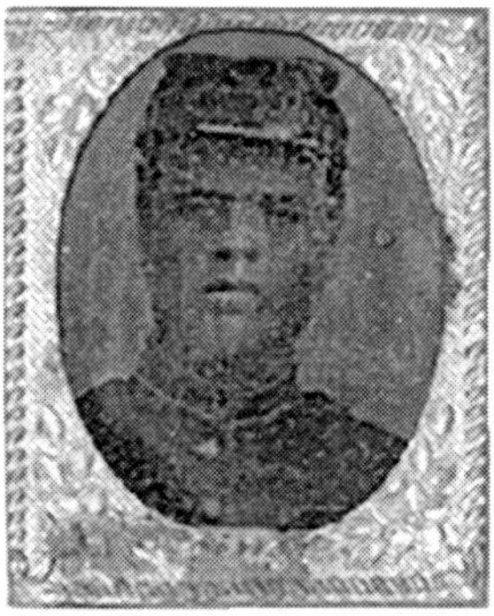

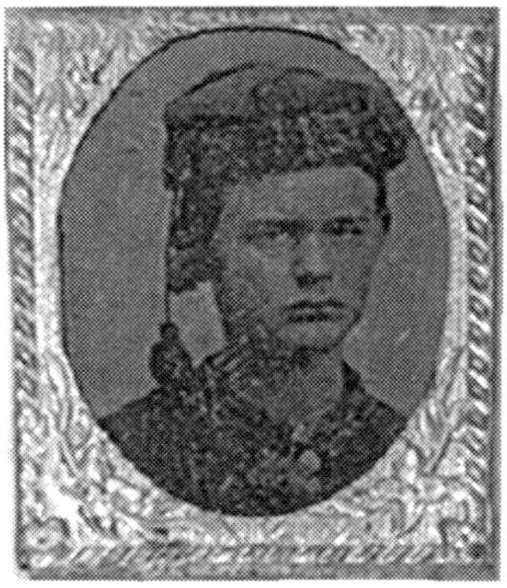

Effie Leatherman

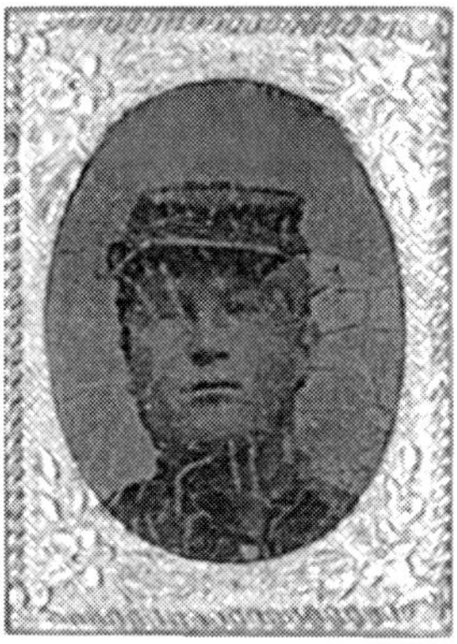

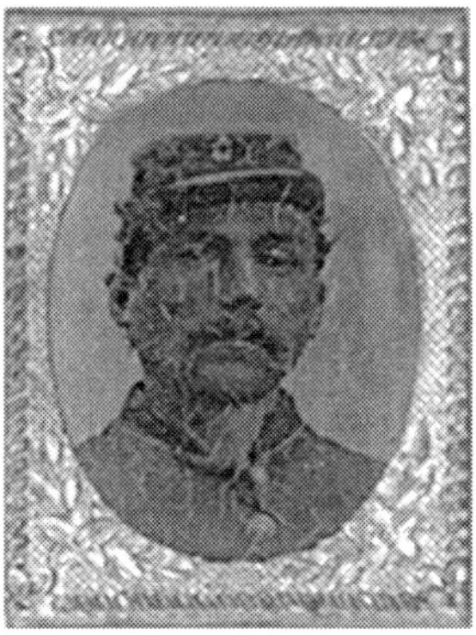

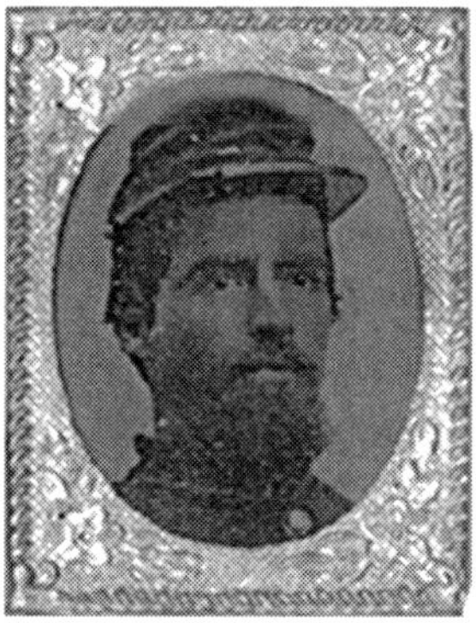

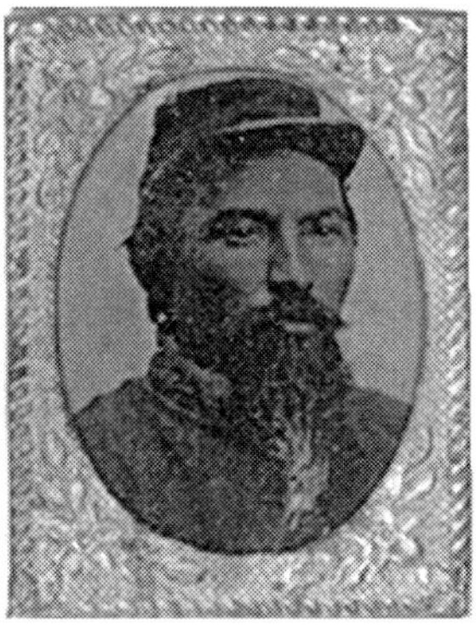

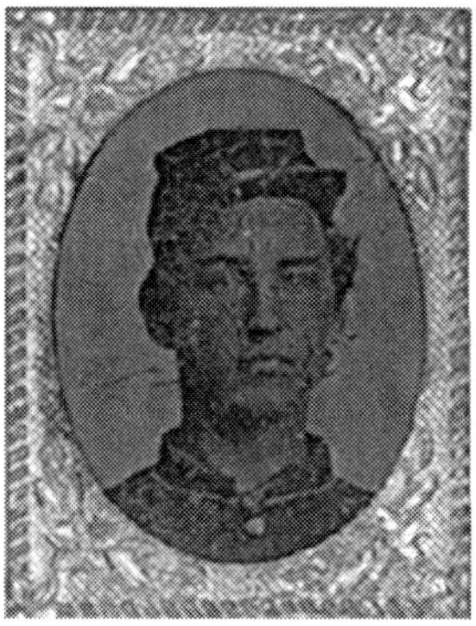

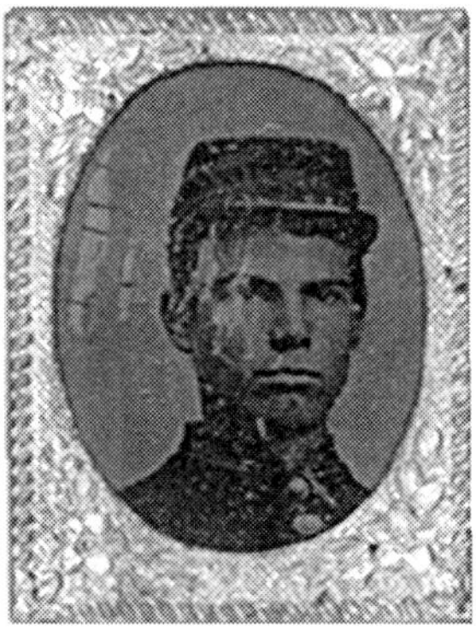

Effie Leatherman

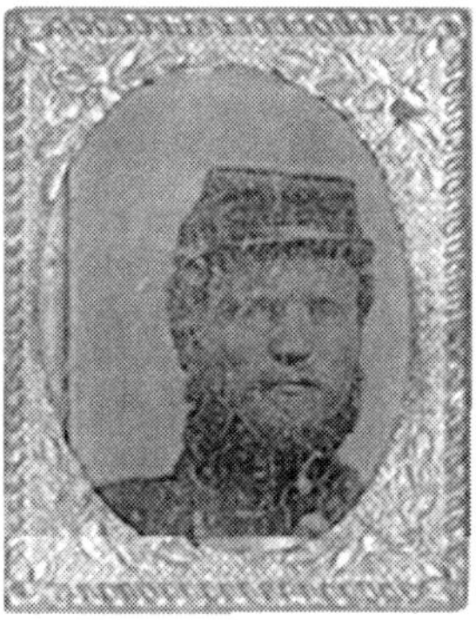

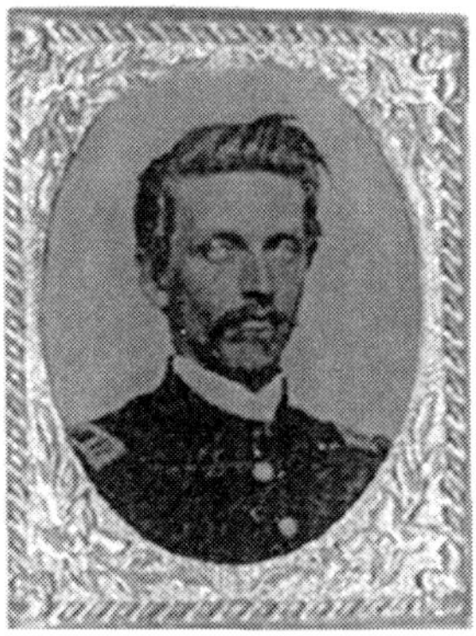

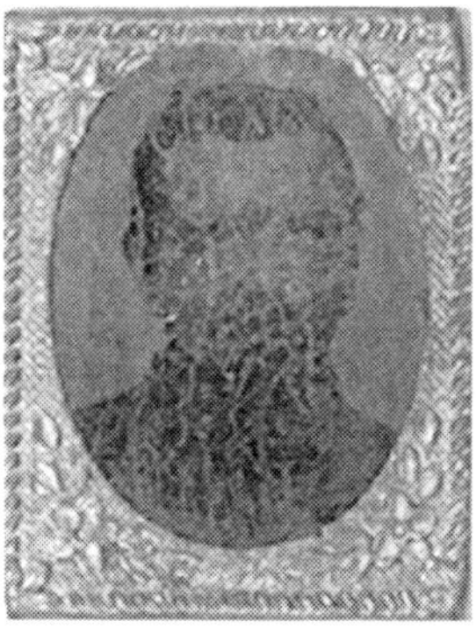

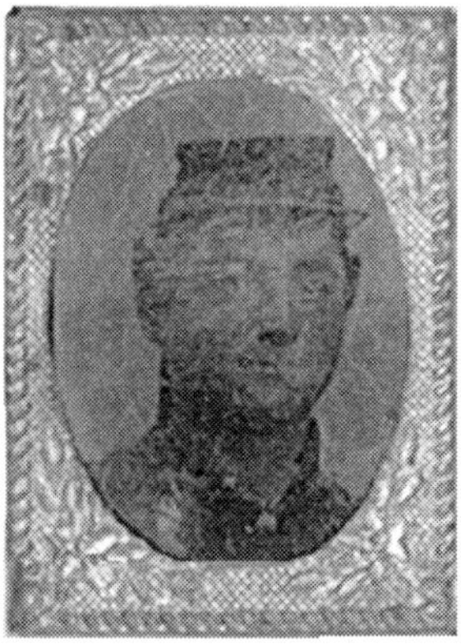

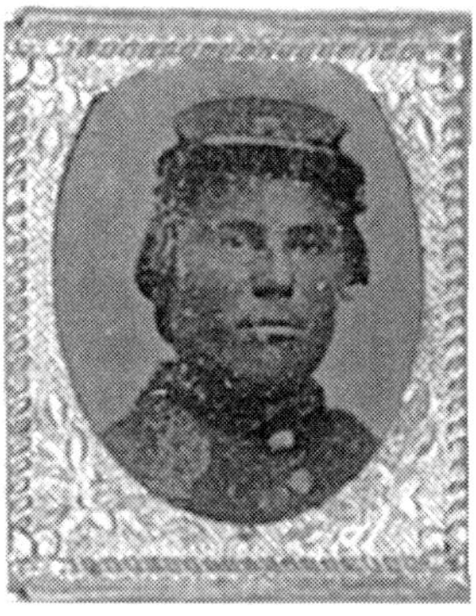

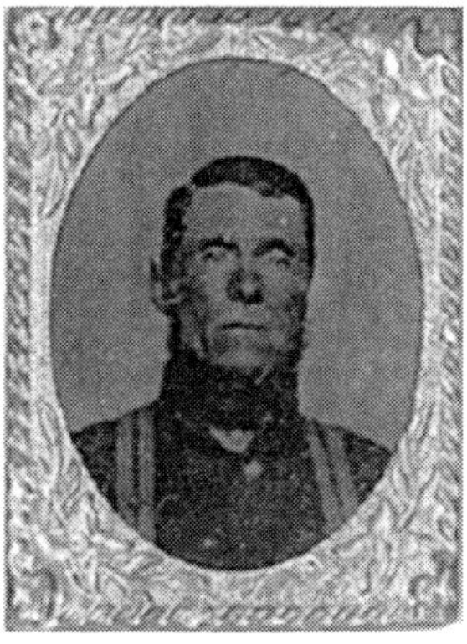

Effie Leatherman

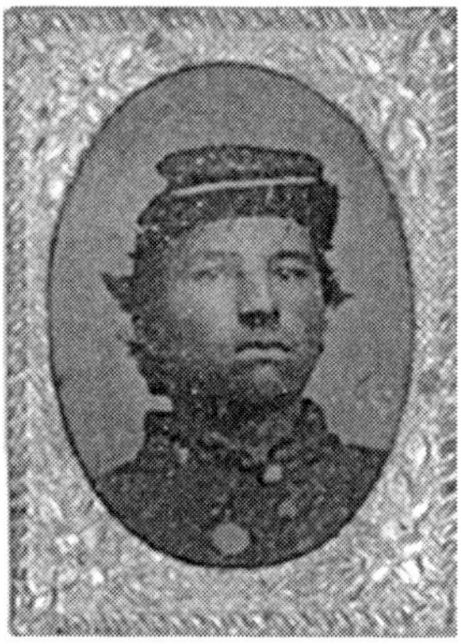

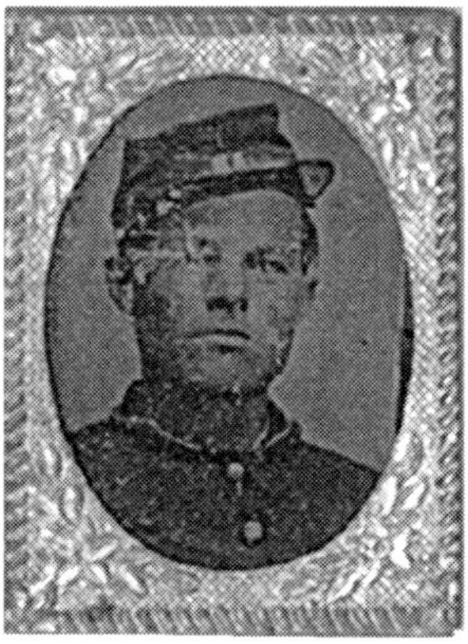

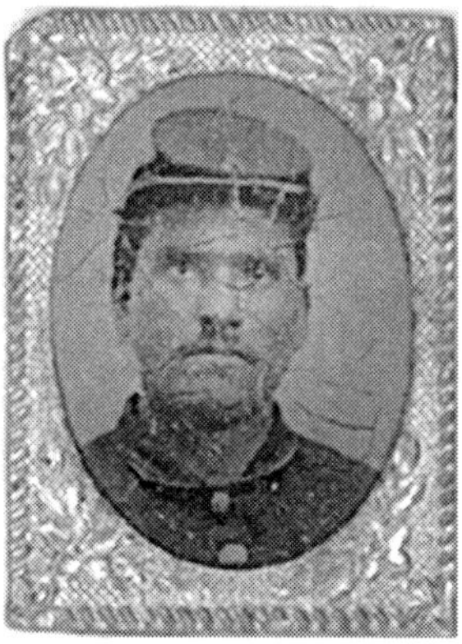

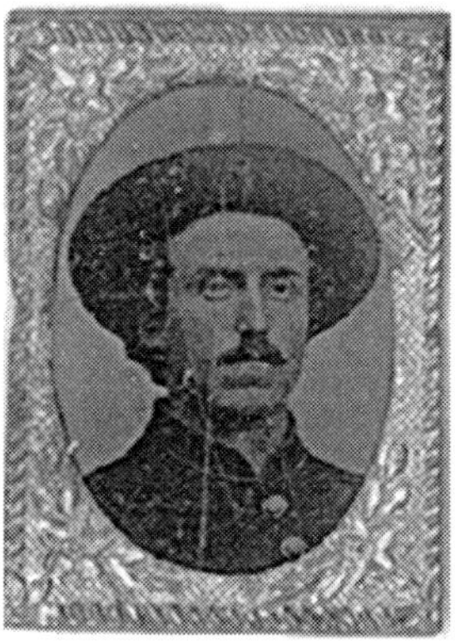

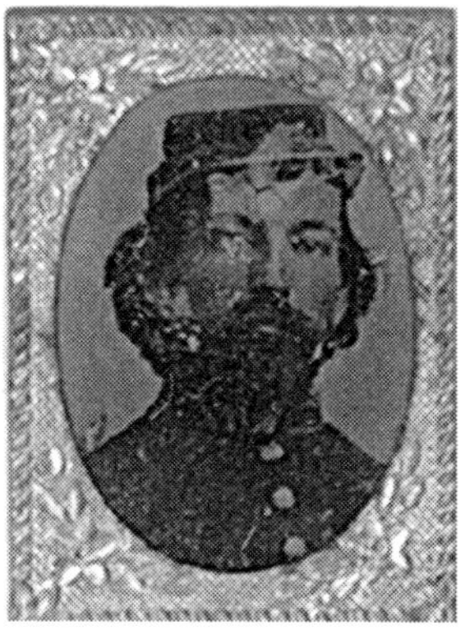

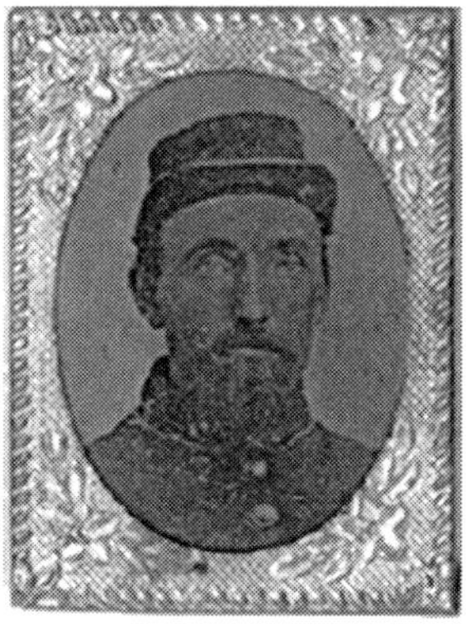

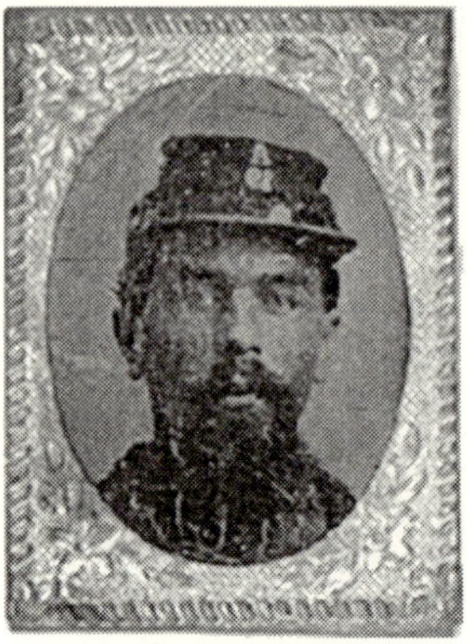

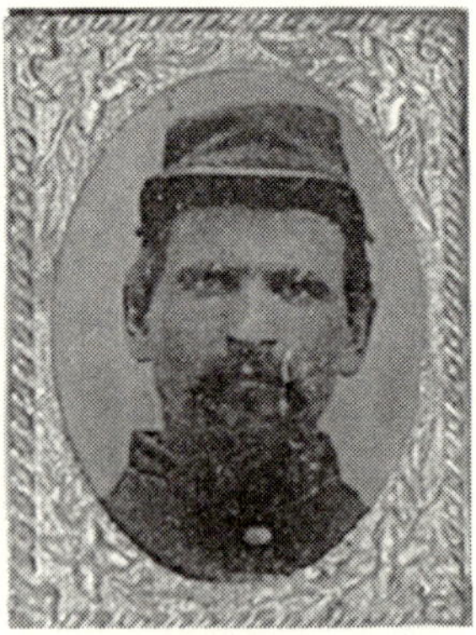

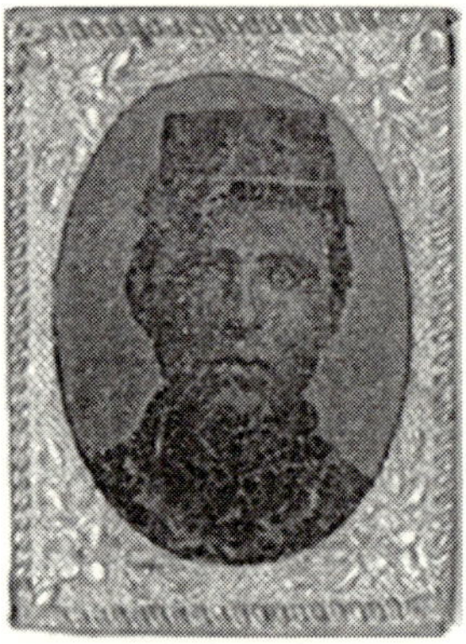

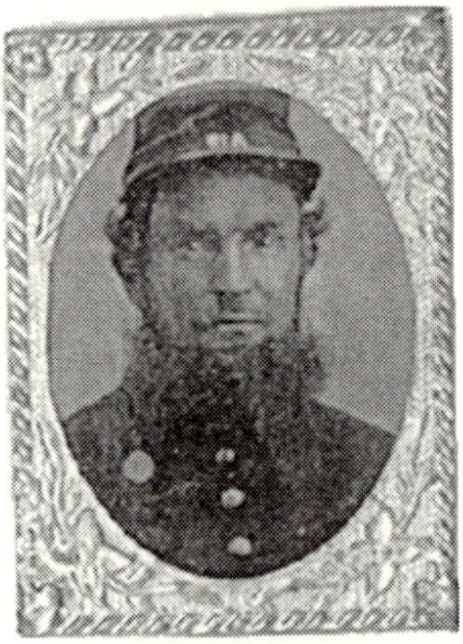

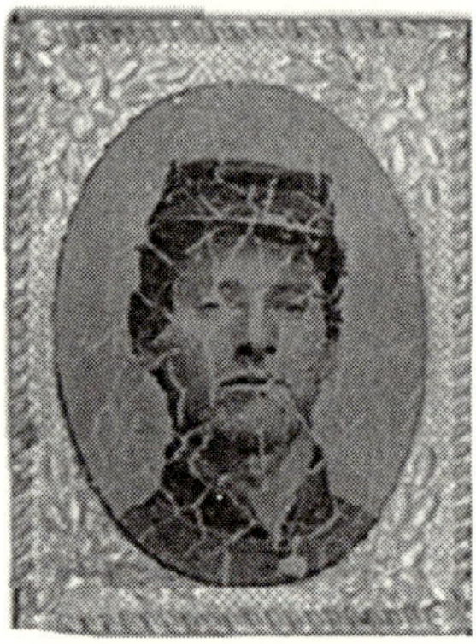

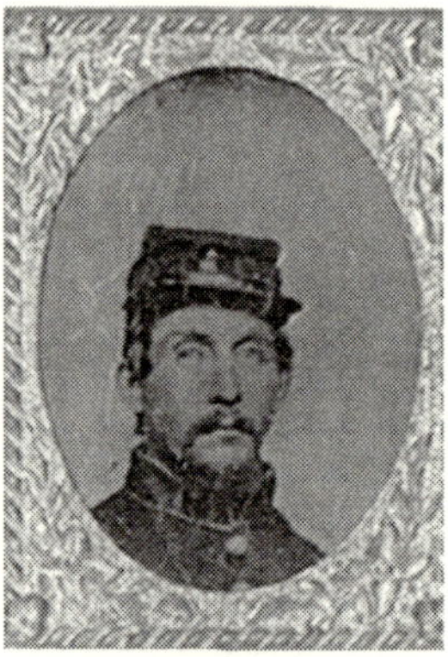

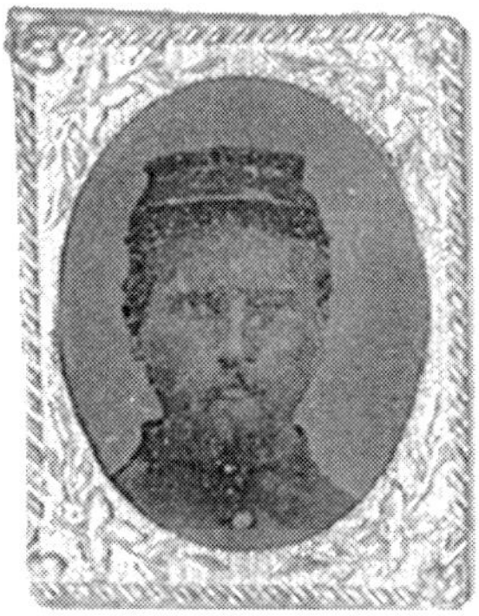

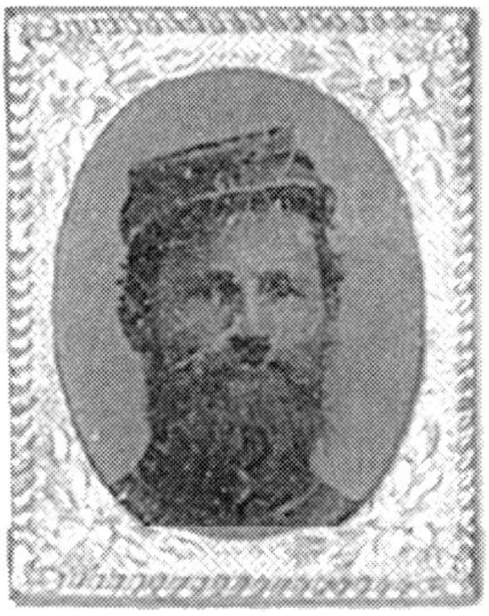

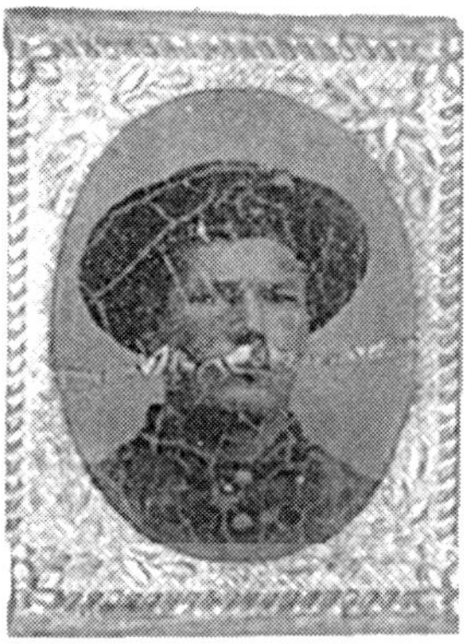

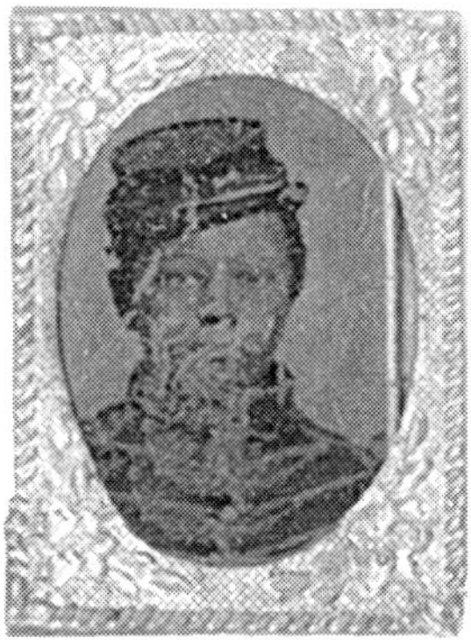

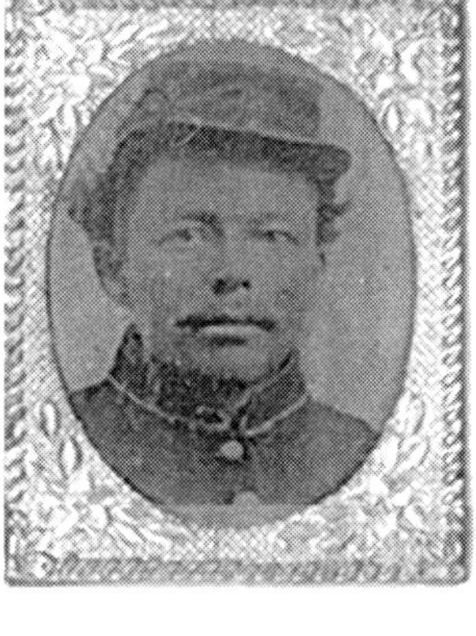

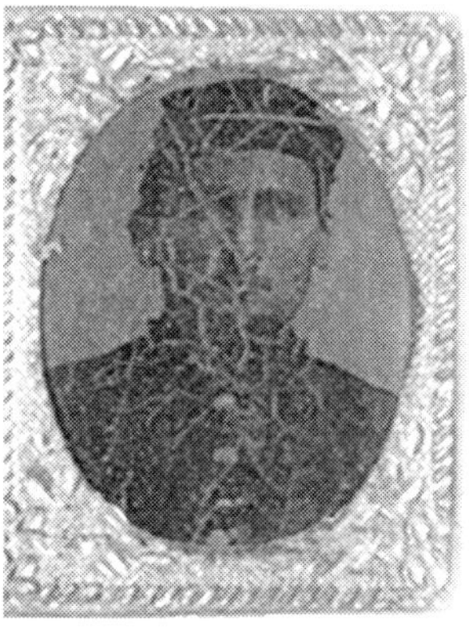

Effie Leatherman

CHAPTER 3

- Private Nelson Slater Gardner

- Diary, April 21, 1864 to November 8, 1864

- Diary, next entry November 9, 1864 to March, 1865 (when paroled)

- Prison History—Ed Curtis

- Prison Life—W.O. Pietzsch

Private Nelson Slater Gardner

Private Nelson Slater Gardner was born January 1, 1846 in PA. When very young he moved to WI, and in December 1861 at the age of 15, he enlisted at Reedsburg, WI in the 19th Regiment of Wisconsin Co. A, Infantry Volunteers and until the following July the regiment acted as guard to Rebel prisoners at Norfolk, VA.

In April of 1863 he was ordered to Suffolk, and many years later given a medal for his heroism when he swam the Nansemond River setting fire to the grasses on the other side to force the Rebels back

December 27, 1863 he was discharged by virtue of reenlistment as a veteran. He stated his age as 20. His enlistment took place in New Bern, North Carolina, and was for a term of three years. His regiment saw service at Petersburg, and the battle of Fair Oaks, VA. He was captured at Richmond, VA on October 27, 1864. It was stated that he was retained in Libby, and Danville prisons, then confined at Salisbury, NC prison for several months.

He was sent to N.E. Ferry, NC, then reported to Camp Parole, MD and Benton Barracks, MO and paroled on May 11, 1865

His diary, written in both pen and pencil began in April 1864 and closed on January 26. 1865. My apologies for any language or racial implications.

Diary, April 21-1864 to November 8, 1864

Thursday, April 21, 1864
I am on gard too day it rained I am on picit board (added note-mending 10 cts)

Saturday, April 23, 1864
I am on gard at head quarters too day and nothing is going on too day worth riting the weather is very warm too day and the farmers is doing thar spring work "that whats the mater so ses Betsey shockingly"

Tuesday April 26, 1864
we left Ewans mill and marched too the camp of

the 19 reg then marched to Fort Spinola and laid on the ground for about 2 hours and marched to the boat called Frances.

Wednesday, April 27, 1864
we are on the boat all day we passed Cape Hatteras about 12 oclock the left wing is on the other boat. they ar on the boat now.

Thursday, April 28, 1864
we landed at Yorktown 3 o'clock A.M. then marched up to sum neighbor houses and stacked arms and laid down for the nit

Friday, April 29, 1864
this morning after breakfast we marched down on the old camp ground on the south side of the fort and after a hel of a long time we pitch our shelter tents and took a rest.

Saturday, April 30, 1864
this morning we mustered for pay and this afternoon we had a general revue the nineth (19th) had a hel of a time. they was a man cum for our company from Camp Randel.

Sunday, May 1, 1864
too day I went down to the town of Yorktown and I express 75 dolars hom today.

Monday, May 2, 1864
I was on guard yesterday it rained for crist sake and I was half lit yesterday on guard at our tent.

Tuesday, May 3, 1864
I was at town too day and cam back and had a batallan drill.

Wednesday, May 4, 1864
We left our camp at Yorktown this morning and took the boat and the cannons over. now on our way to Fort Monroe we land I dont no (know)
.

Thursday, May 5, 1864
We left Fort Monroe to day about 12 o'clock and we landed at City Point at 11:00 o'clock

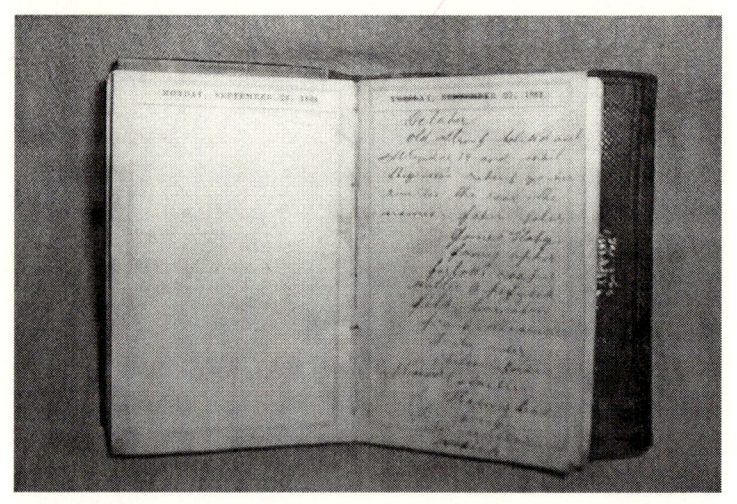

Friday, May 6, 1864
I am at old Bermuda Hundred too day and our regiment has got out on the firing too day and they will have a hel of a fit (fight) too morrow.

Monday, May 9, 1864
too day we left our camp and started for the field

and we marched about 2 miles and then our company started out as a skirmish and then we stad (stayed) out and stad out till 12 o'clock then we laid in the shad for a while then the Captain called me and I started far ahead and then slept in the gearson with him.

May 12, 1864
we left camp this morning with 2 days rashans (rations) and we marched 8 miles and then we came to the turn pik thar we found our men dead and burned then we marched on and cam too a field and ther we laid down for a half hour and then we marched thro the tufis (toughest) hils that I ever saw.

Friday, May 13, 1864
our company went out skirmished all day and I was on the left of our company and a had a hel of a tim. We fell back and then Baxter had orders too take the brick house and he started out with seven men too tak the house and took it post haste and without fits (fights) and ended purty bad

Sunday, May 15, 1864
and ther we found the Rebels as thick as the devil then we laid down for the evening.
this morning our company formed out as skirmishes and then we marched on till we found the Rebels and then I went out as skirmisher and then the Rebels fired in thar for sum time and the Rebels charged on us and then they fell back

and then a bullet hit and Capt Pits (Pitts) was wounded.

May 17, 1864
this morning we left our camp har we stad (where we stayed) for the nit and went down too a piece of woods and thar we laid till nit and the shell and shot came whislin and killed many and wounded Cap before they moved him too the hospital he died. Bob Sawyer was wounded in the nit.

May 18, 1864
this morning our company went out on picket and then the bullets flew like hal and thar we remanded for the nit

May 19, 1864
this morning we was attacked an the Rebels dove into the refill (rifle) pits and then the fit (fight) comments and then the Rebels forged on us and then our men ran like the devil and our men got wounded lik everything but I can't member thar names now John Fosnot he was one they was 8 men in all.

Monday, May 23, 1864
too day we left our camp this morning we left for camp for picting (picketing) and I am on a (never finished)

Tuesday, May 24, 2864
to day we drew our pay. I am at work too day.

Tuesday, May 31, 1864
too day I am on gard too the wharf and garding hurd tack and oats and whil I was hear this morning I saw a calvary man with two sea sick they are calvary regiment light calvary regiment here "that what the mater so says Betsy shockingly"

June l, 2864
too day I am on gard the Rebels and our picit had a fit (fight) last nit

June 2, 1864
too day it is very wrm (warm) and the sun shines as wrm as a cook oven and in the afternoon it comments raining and it rained all nit we went down too the dock and unloaded sum wounded men and one Reb. he was wounded pirty bad. John was tid up all nit. (?)

Saturday, June 4, 1864
too day I lay in camp and at nit I went on picit and it coments raining all nit and all quiet. no gun heard on picit

Sunday, June 5, 1864
this morning it rained still and I may be put on the relief

(no date) I received five dolars from Henry Craft for washing

Tuesday, June 7, 1864
too day I was in the camp all day and I went on picit guard too nit and we had a heavy heart too nit when we mounted gard I dru sum clos (clothes) too day I am reserv picit for too nit

Wednesday, June 8, 1964
I have been on gard all day and I am a gentry (going to) stay all nit our regiment releaved the 62 Ohio and I think they are going to hav sum fun to nit so no more at present rit soon.

Thursday 9, 1864
all day they hav been heavy firing on the gun boat and they hav made the Rebels git and they ar still firing yet and I think they will take the fort too nit I think

Sunday, June 12, 1864
too day I hav ben in camp all day and they had inspection about 12 oclock and I dont no when they will go on psicit (picket) or not they have ben 2 reddyment of 100 days men in camp of Ohio troops that is all this time rit soon

Monday, June 13, 1864
last nit our company and other companys went on picit and I was on reserve last nit and this morning my self and Henry Streat was on post too geather the Rebels had been throwing sheal (shell) and the railroad iron at our men we ar on the north side of the slu (slough) and the rest of our company ar on the reserve we will be releaved too nit if nothing happens

Tuesday, June 14, 1864
too day I lay in camp all day and too nit report for picit whar for I dont no now I hav found I am on at the brk (break) of day

Wednesday, June 15, 1864
well I have been on gard all day and now I am going to be releaved the 18 army corps went to Petersburg last nit this morning they was heavy firing in that direction how it cam out I dont no it

Thursday, June 16, 1864
too day I lay in camp this for noon then our company had orders to go out and reconnaissance (not his spelling) out on the railway and we went out and blew the rail gard up and rased hell

Friday, June 17, 1864
too day I lay in camp all day our company has ben on picit too nit and I remain in camp too nit and now am in the rifil (rifle) pits looking for what I can cover Carder is hear too day it has been very warm too day I hav riten (written) a letter hom too day for the first time in a long time

Saturday, June 18, 1864
I am in camp too day we have laid in the breast work all day about I hurd that Petersburg was taken and then I hurd it counterdicked our company come from picit too nit all was well.

Sunday, June 19, 1864
too day it was warm and we had too inspections too day and then we mounted gard for picit too nite and then we was sent back all but Hugh Cohans behind he went on picket and I say booly for him.

Monday, June 20, 1864
that I dont much mis the gard too day I am in camp the day all day nither the company has been on picit too nit but I remain in camp all day I had a swim too day that all

Tuesday, June 21, 1864
last nit our redlyment (regiment) left our camp and reported at General Butler quarters and then this morning we started for the armery at Petersburg and we started at 4 oclock and we march till noon and now we ar in a field of oats

and about 1 mile from Petersburg I don't no what is a goin to happen and I dont cair (care) what

Wednesday, June 22, 1864
last nit I marched too this place about 1 half mil from Petersburg Jess Mallow was wounded too day it is so dark that I cant see too rit.

Thursday, June 23, 1864
too day we lay in the rifel pits they sheld (shelled) us sum and shot thar shell like fun and we lay till nit and then we was releaved by the infrantry heavy artilery and was marched too the rear down in the holar near a crick and thar we lay till morning

Friday, June 24, 1864
too day we lay in a revean (revine) and this morning the Rebels thored (throwed) thar shells rit over in the revean whar we lay and wounded Ogall Oganunery and now we ar going sum whoir (where) the whole garison ar under marching orders I rot (wrote) a leter hom too day.

Saturday, June 25, 1864
too day we lay in camp all day and the shell coim (came) in rit smart today we hav got marchin orders and I think that we air going in the frunt lin of brest work and now we ar going now

Sunday, June 26, 1864
too day I am in the Rebel pits and they thro thear (their) shell lik fun the sharp shoters shoot in lik

the devel the Rebels trid (tried) our lines last nit but they got plaid (played) out and had too back rapidly and shoot very shaby

Monday, June 27, 1864
all is quit (quiet) now hear now all but a fair deal firing on the lines hear nun (none) is hurt that no one noes (knows) any more at present

Tuesday, June 28, 1864
too day ant anything going on hear at present too day I saw a man woulded (wounded) too day rit behind mi tent he was cuting up meat and he was wounded rit thar and he fell rit on the ground the order is to pack up and fall in and moov (move) at dusk and I dont no whair (where) and I dont cair

Wednesday, June 29, 1864
we air in the rifle pits all day we cam last nit they advance our picit line last nit
Fulvester was kiled too day he was shot rit thur (threw) the head and now he is dead and they have been to bary (bury) him he was shot thru the head and he was reading a paper

Thursday, June 30, 1864
too day I am with the rigment too day in the rifil (rifle) pits and we mustered for pay too day and about 3 ocloock in the afternoon they had a fit (fight) Captain Nickels and Corpel Gats are dead and so about thrity of his men was dead all was nigers killed with a shell it is reported that the nigers took a fort too day

Friday, July 1, 1864
too day we lay in the rifel pits all day not nearly firing goin on too day I expect that we will be relieved too nit

Saturday, July2, 1864
last nit we was relieved from the rifel pits and then we marched to our camp in the holar and thar we lay for the nit and then this morning we marched up the revean and thar we lay for the day.

Sunday, July 3, 1864
too day our regiment lay in camp too day and Hollinghead (Pvt. John) had a whisk of a gin we had all the bru that we could drink we had a whisky rashen too nit we ar packing up too nit for the frunt too not whar I dont no

Monday, July 4, 1864
I hav ben in the frunt line of rifel pits too day all day and they hant bin much firing on the line too day it has bin a day for the artelry (artillery) hav ben a good deal of shelling goin last nit

Tuesday, July 5, 1864
I hav been in the rifel pits all day and they hav been very quiet too day Walas Holton (Wm W.) was wounded too day with a shell I think that we will be relieved we believe that will be ordered to nit all to nit it is hot too day hear Eprum was wounded in the rit sid (right side)

Wednesday, July 6, 1864
too day I lay in camp nothing goin on too day
too mount too any I borid (borrowed) 5 dolars off
Cooper too day (George W. Cooper)

Thursday, July 7, 1864
I am in camp too day nothing goin on I saw
Cashis too day shot a burly Welsh too day I think
that we will go on the frunt too nit I saw a fit
(fight) in the regiment

Friday, July 8, 1964
We air in the rifel pits we cam last nit they hav
been a good deal firing on the frunt line too day
we air on the reserve line too day

Saturday, July 9, 1864
too day I lay in the rifel pits all day nothing going
on too day not much firing on the frunt we will be
relieved too nit

Sunday, July 10, 1864
I had orders this morning to pack up and git redy
for a march too day it has been very warm we had
inspection this morning

Monday, July 11, 1864
I hav been in camp too day we drad oats for today
I was detailed today for frunt gard and we go out
too nit but I dont no what is our duty if yet they
ar a grat (great) deal of shelling going on hear
now they ar releaving picit too nit the Rebels are
putting the shell in lik hell it looked lik rain too
nit the wind is blowing lik fun

Tuesday, July 12, 1864
I hav been on front gard too day for the first tim and I lik it they had ben shooting on the frunt (front) they are shelling now our men wounded too day in both of our redgment

Wednesday, July 13, 1864
too day they hant much firing in the front too day I think that we will be relieved too nit it is quiet still the frunt now no one hurt in our redgment that I no too day

Thursday, July 14, 1864
I hav been on gard too day garding a corn field too keep the men from shoting in the corn. I found Cashs Holons (Charles) too day

Friday, July 15, 1864
I am laying in camp too nit and lad all day doing nothing I bard (borrowed) 5.00 off Capt Laton too day I will be on the frunt too nit

Saturday, July 16, 1864
today I hav ben hear all day doing nothing I hav a easy tim I saw E L Farmer too day and he is on duty in the holar he is slitly (slightly) wounded.

Sunday, July 17, 1864
too day I am in the road here doing nothing mor than yourself we ar too be relieved too nit Sargent Numan of company P was slitly wounded he was standing in the corn field hiching (hitching) up his pants and the ball took him in the sid slitly and made him holar holar lik the devil

Monday, July 18, 1864
too day I lay in camp too day and I am on gard
too today and I stood at rest and too nit I am titer
than a wild owl

Tuesday, July 19, 1864
too day I lay in camp all day and rained lik fun
it rained all day and ar regement worked all nit
lifting down sum breast works and too nit we will
go out in the pits too nit

Wednesday, July 20, 1864
too day i am in the rear of the brigade and our
regiment is on the frunt line on the schirmish
line and Carigan of the drum corp was wounded
then in the arm and Jimbus of a r g was wounded
thru the arm wrist this fore noon our regiment
changed prisoners with the Rebels Millard (Pvt.
Eliezer Millard) and (Franklin) Winchester from
our company.

Thursday, July 21, 1864
too day I lay behind mi brest work all day there
was a man wounded in our regiment too day we
will be releaved too nit

Friday, July 22, 1864
too day I am in camp too day nothing going as
I am a gard and got lit and I got hell and all
rit I got a letter from father and he sent me a
silk handcheaf and I had one from Gardner too
(possibly brother).

Saturday, July 23, 1864
too day I am in camp too day but will go out on the frunt too nit my old head feals lik a whiskey cast.

Sunday, July 24, 1864
too day I lay in the road all day doing nothing too mount too we think its raining now not very hard have ben on guard too day

Monday, July 25, 1864
too day we lay in the road in the rear of our brigade doing nothng more than the day before we are too be releaved too nit and go too our camp they ar shelllng lik fun we had a hell of a rain last nit

Tuesday, July 26, 1864
too day lay in camp all day doing nothing went about 2 miles after green apels (apples) our ridgement had dress parade and Ephram and I had a hel of a time

Wednesday, July 27. 1864
too day I hav ben on gard too day nothng nu our ridlement is gong out too nit and the former gard is gong out but am gong too stay n too nit for sumthng (something) but don't know what for

Thursday, July 28, 1864
too day I lay in camp all day was out too gard this mornng am on gard to the comersare (commisary too nit the molasses got splt (spilt) last nit Teater (1st LT Henry A. Tator) hurld (heard) a fus last nit

Friday, July 29, 1864
too day I hav been in camp all day and our brgad (brigade) has marchng orders they ar ordered too pack up and be ready too march at dark wth 2 days rashens in ther haver sacks

Saturday, July 30, 1864
last nit we left our camp and we went down on the left and sporten (supporting) the calvary and we blu (blew) up a fort and it had four hundred darkies in it and it kilt every one of them and this coor has been in camp and I am left too gard the others dont no our troops charged the Rebel works and cared (carried) them

Sunday, July 31, 1864
this mornng we left our camp and went out in the hils in the rear of our brgad I hav been on gard all the whil

Monday, August 1, 1864
too day we lay in the rear line of rifl pits on duty it is as still as I ever heard it since I hav been here it is reported that Pits (Newman Pitts) has com from the hospital but I havent saw him yet

Tuesday, August 2, 1864
I hav ben on the reserve too day all day and too this evenng I went down and saw Cassius Colons he was all rit he was in that charg and cam out all rit

Wednesday, August 3, 1864
too day I have ben dong nothng for a good whil

too nit we go in camp when I went in camp I saw John Fosnot he was well all rit

Thurday, August 4, 1864
I now ar on post gardng the corn field keepng the boys from maneuvering (not his spelling) it I had a tit with the main burners what else I dont no I am siting under a peach tree riting our regment is having inspechin (inspection)

Friday, August 5, 1864
I am in camp too day but think that we will go too the frunt too nit they ar a good deal of talk of us gong hom on a vertrun (veteran) furlow but dont no how tru it is for we cant tell what is gong on for you will hear all sorts of reports I saw Rusel Readpel (Russell Redfield) here was up to our company too day and the hours go by

Saturday, August 6, 1864
too day we lay in the rear of our brest work dong nothing but keep the men from goin too the rear I understand that there was a man wounded too in company C last nit Clarence A. Danforth was mortly wounded the bool (ball) went into his shoulder and came out of his bowels dont no how he is

Sunday, August 7, 1864
I am in the rear of the brigad and we expect that we will go in too nit this morning Robert Cheek was killed he was hit in the head and did (died) in about 2 hours after he hit

Monday, August 8, 1864
too day I have ben in camp most all day but Crosher and I had sum good fun at nit Old Carnel (Colonel) Strom cald (called) up the veterans and they voted too go hom and I think they will

Tuesday, August 9, 1864
too day I am on gard and our ridgment has ben out too the frunt I dont go I found Geo Chelsa Gardner

Wednesday, August 10, 1864
too day they havt ben much going on hear our ridgment is out to the frunt yet

Thursday, August 11, 1864
too day I have been un well all day our ridyment will be relieved too nit if nothng hapens.

Friday, August 12, 1864
too day was releaved from provo duty and we expect too start for hom too morrow

Saturday, August 13, 1864
too day I hav had the fevor all day and at 5 p.m. we fell in and marched to City Point and thar we reman til morning

Sunday, August 14, 1864
this morning at 10 oclock we left City Point on the Lory Vanderbilt and landed at Fort Manroe at 4 oclock then we got on the bot Fort Washington left Port Monroe haft past 5 oclock Norfolk and landed at half past 6 oclock and marched at the rear of the Andrews House (?) and thar lay for the nit

Monday, August 15, 1864
too day hav ben layng round the City of Norfolk we hant got any pay yet

Tuesday, August 16, 1864
too day they hant been much going on hear the wether is very warm I havnt been well too day

Wednesday, August 17, 1864
too day I have ben runnng around town and three oclock cam and we left Norfolk for Baltimore

Monday, August 22, 1864
this mornng we eat breakfast and then I got in

the ambulance and went up too Camp Randall and thar went in the hospital and hear I am

Tuesday, August 23, 1864
too day I am in the hospital laying on mi cot but I had sum liker too drink

Wednesday, August 24, 1864
too day I am in the hospital but was down in too a saloon and got purty tit and then went too the hospital and I spuk (puke) for cris sake too nit is pay rol but havent gotin pay yet.

Nothng more until October-appears to be on furlough

Sunday, October 2, 1864
too day I ate mi dinner at our hotel and then we went to Weaver house and ther I left the old foks and then went too Baraboo and then Walter A. Pietzsch and I went out and saw the girls

Monday, October 3, 1864
this mornng I left Baraboo for Madison in a four horse team and we had a old tim we got in Madison at dusk and thar I saw____and we had sum fun you may bet

Tuesday, October 4, 1864
last nit I went too the theator and then we went back up too the tavern at the Maiream (?) and then we went to Camp Randel and then went

down to the city again and went too a circus and staid in the city that nit and went too camp in the morning.

Wednesday, October 5, 1864
this morning I cam from the sity (city) and we drad our board money and then we went to the city and I got drunker than a fool and our regiment lit here about 10 oclock at nit and we had a hel of a time

Thursday, October 6, 1864
this morning we arrived in Klgo (Chicago) at day lit and then changed cars and started and I got left at Fort Wan (Wayne, Ind.) and I laid over till 12 oclock at nit then I got transportaton.

Friday, October 7, 1864
and I rad all day and at nit I arrived in Pittsburg at nit and after we got about half way the train ahead of us run off the track and raised hel I slept at the hostell at the deepo all nit

Saturday, October 8, 1864
in the morning we started out for our breakfast and then we lay around town all day I an Dirus Cidder was with me at nit we put up too the tavern we went too the provo marshall and then got us a pass till Monday morning at 10 oclock

Sunday, October 9, 1864
and ths mornng we started out for breakfast an Yousel (?) and ther we stay around town tll about

3 oclock n the afternoon then the First Wisconsin heavy artillry cam aboard and I got on with them and started for Dca (DC)

Monday, October 10, 1864
and this morning we arrived at Harrisburg and then we stayed till 1 oclock in the afternoon and then we started southward for Boltmoor (Baltimore)and then we got ther at dark and then we went too the solders hom and thar we got our supper and then we went to the tavern stayed all nit

Tuesday, October 11. 1864
this morning we took breakfast at the soldiers hom and then we went and reported too the Provo Marshall and he sent us up to Camp dstrbuchon (distribution) and 1 oclock we started for Fort Monroe and we got another boat Canoeps (?) and every other thing and we road all nit and crowded up like hogs

Wednesday, October 12, 1864
We rode all day on the water and all nit without anything to eat and hardly too eat.

Thursday, October 13, 1864
 goti n Fort Monroe at 10 oclock in the mornng and then was sent to Norfolk and then saw the ___and went to City Point and came back and with Bill Willhand

Friday, October 14, 1864
This morning took breakfast and had mi likness taken (picture) and then got mi transportaton and started for Fort Monroe for the frunt

Saturday, October 15, 1864
this mornng I left Fort Monroe for the frunt and now am gong up to Burmuda Hundred thats what the mater

Sunday, October 16, 1864
last nt slep at ___ _____and then started for the frunt from Bermuda Hundred I got too the frunt about 4 oclock and was all well and mi nap sack was sent to the rear but it is cold as thunder

Thursday, October 27, 1864
this morning we left our camp whar we lay for the nit and started in the morning before day lit for the rit of our line and we marched 25 miles and we cam to Far Oaks what the Rebels call 7 Pines and thar we found the Rebels is in a fort and brest works and our old birgad had ordered to tak it and Ole Steng (Strong) hollered out "surrender 19" and while they was taking us we run to the rear and thar we was taken prisoner

Friday, October 28, 1864
too day am siting in Lily prison sucking my claws but I am all rit but how long I will be I dont no but think I am a _____for the time at best I think that I will haf too try it at all times

Saturday, October 29. 1864
too day I still remain in prison in the sam manner but feal purty well and think that I will com out all rit after awhile but not fret the catch

Sunday, October 30, 1864
notng nu but the grub has first com in by too big nigers carng it over a towel one peas (piece) of corn bread and a peas of meat not any salt on it and we hav that twice a day wel we can liv on that at lest we will hav too.

Tuesday, November 1, 1864
too day they hant much gong on but the same over and over every day it is a hungry tim hear now but I think that thar ar a beter day comin I hope in every way at nit is the coldst time we have I hant got any clothes what I have got and but I think (not finished)

Thursday, November 3, 1864
too day am in prison at Lily and it is raining lik fun and it is very cold in this room and the boys ar walkng too ceap (keep) warm and sum ar laying down and others are playing cards whil others are smoking and the sam every day.

Friday, November 4, 1864
this mornng we left Lily prison and we took the cars for Sailsbury and this morning it rained like hel and we got in sum catel (cattle) cars and we drew 2 days rashens and the meat stunked lik fun and no man could eat it.

Saturday, November 5, 1864
we rode all day and we arrived at Greensboro and thar we lay in the cars for sum time and then the gard marched us in too a big field and thar we lay all nit wthout any thing to eat or hardly an fir or any blankets spread over us

Sunday, November 6, 1864
and this morning we marched down to the train and then we started for Salisbery, North Carolin and then we started and rad all day till nit with out anything too eat yet and then at dark we got too our journey at dark and they put us in a big pen and thar we stad for the nit

Monday, November 7, 1864
and this morning wee got up out of the mud and bout ten oclock we got a half pint of soop for the first time since we left Richmond

Tuesday, November 8, 1864
too day I am in camp garded by the Rebels and the pen that I am in is the dirtis hall that any human being ever was in crist time and it rained all the whil and it rains now and it is all mud and water now and still running over vats _____ is out today and the rest of the solgers (soldiers) must make it up.

Diary, next entry November 9, 1864 to March, 1865 (when paroled)

Wednesday, November 9, 1864
this holy day I am in this prison camp nothing going on here today but it is a hungry tim and mudy and "hard times I should call it if I was a sitison (citizen) but that I am a solger (soldier) I call it midlin times" and tho it is the tuffis tim that I ever saw in my lif and I will never see such a tim again in mi lif but I don't no about it they say we were going too see the sun for the first tim since wee hav ben here

Thursday, November 10, 1864
too day is a pirty (pretty) day and too day I got a half lof of bread and I feel quite revived last nit it rained some too day it is clear but it is a hungry tim hear now but beter times is coming we have rolcall but we ar prisoner of war at prison camp at Salisbery, North Carolina

Friday, November 11, 1864
Prisoner of War at Salisbery, North Carolina
well too day I hav had a midlin good time. too day this weather is pirty fair now but last nit it was rather cold but we got a _____first rate

considering we ar gettin meal pur man too nit
and the sargent is going round with salt for the
first time

Saturday, November 12, 1864
too day is a cold ray day the wind blas cold and
the air is cold too day. I drad about a spoons full
of ris (rice) and the well has ben dry and we hav
got the ris dry yet and we will hav to cook our
grub in the morning last nit it was so cold that
they was men found dead siting up and sum
found in ther burths dead and other almost dead
they dy from 20 to 25 a day hear

Sunday, November 13, 1864
Salisbery, North Carolina
I am siting in mi nest and it is cold and last nit
was a cold nit you may bet they was 13 men found
ded (dead) this morning around firs (fires) and in
thar siting nests and the rumor is too day that
were to exchanged in a fu days but I don't beav
(believe) it for they ar a many storys that you cant
believe them

Monday, November 14, 1864
Prisner of war in Salsbery, North Carolina
well too day has ben a midlin warm day but too
nit is cold enuff (enough) too make it all up too no
more at present from Nelson Gardner

Tuesday, November 15, 1864
too day other boys in mi tent and mi self fixt up
the tent as warm as we can they ar four of us and
all we hav too cover us is a peas of carpit and that

bout big enugg too cover us but we will hav too make the best of it we can the boys is siting all the tim

(my notes) "Reports have been told of the local citizens cutting up the carpets in the church and their homes and passing pieces over the fence to the prisoners."

Wednesday, November 16, 1864
Prisner of War in Salsbery, North Carolina
well too day I havt felt very well but I hope that I will fel better too morrow. I hav had the diree (diarrhea) too day but it is giting better now I hav hurd (heard) too day that all the working men is ordered in camp to nit for they ar a gonty (going to) send us away but I dont beleav it I am willing too bee sent any tim

Thursday, November 17, 1864
Prisner of War in Salsbery, North Carolina
Prisoner of War is the dandies(dangist) hole that ever was in North Carolin but they ar grat talk of exchanin us but I dont beleav what I hear we har they hav all sorts of reports but too day it is quite warm

Friday, November 18, 1864
Prisner of War in Salsbery, North Carolina
too day is a pirty por tim hear but it is a midlin camp here but they dont much going on hear too day it is very ungelthy (unhealthy) hear but I think that we can stand it it rains and rains and still raining they was forty died last nit

Saturday, November 19, 1864
Prisner of War at Salsbery, North Carolina
this morning it comenst raining and it rained all day and it is cold as the devel and we havnt had anything to eat yet.

Sunday, November 20, 1864
Prisner of War at Salsbery, North Carolina
it is still raining and drisling all the time when it quit raining I dont no our tent fell down last nit but I think that this is a hell of a place but that I dont kow the worst rain, and they about 40 died last nit

Monday, November 21, 1864
Prisner of War at Salsbery, North Carolina
it is raining and it has been raining for three days and our tent has run full of water they was one man killed last nit and one wounded by the gard they hav shot a good many of our troups it is the darndis hole that I ever saw it is still raining and God nose when it is a going stop for I dont

Tuesday, November 22, 1864
Prisoner of War in Salsbery, North Carolina
well it has stoped raining and it is colder than Greenland the wind is in the north and the ground is froson fast it is unsbelthy (unhealthy) hear for a day it is raining and the next day it freezing and hailing and blasing (blowing) it is cold now but I think it wont last long

Wednesday, November 23, 1864
Prisner of War in Salsbery, North Carolina
this day is litel warmer and not very warm after all last nit was a very cold nit and too nit would bee any warmer but I got along very well last nit if they wood giv us nuff wood to burn I woodnt mind it but we arnt allowed to send only four men out after wood in a day too last one hundred and five men har prisoners

Thursday, November 24, 1864
Prisner of War in Salsbery, North Carolina
in this pen whar we hav to stay I hav washed once for the first time in a good whil too day is Thanksgiving day they say last nit was cold nit you may bet I traded mi pants last nit for a Rebel par of pants and I luk (look) lik the devel we drad quarter rashens this morning but I think that we will dra mor the next tim

Friday, November 25, 1864
Prisner of War in Salsbery, North Carolina
this day has ben a tuff old day we was building our chimbly (chimney) and they was a riet (riot) in camp and they was making a brak and they rarad (paraded) around for som tim before they got quieted down and they was sum got out and they was men cild (killed) and a bout forty wounded and the boys got the guns from sum of the gards and rased hel with things

Saturday, November 26, 1864
Prisner of War in Salsbery, North Carolina

this morning we drad quarter rashan and I dont
no whether we will dra any mor too day or not but
I think that we will mak a go of it but it is hunger
times hear I got a pint of ris (rice) this morning
for two dolars a cup

Sunday, November 27, 1864
Prisner of War at Salsbery, North Carolina
well too day is a fogy day and we drad half
rashons too day drad some meat and ris (rice) and
they havnt ben saying too day lik they hav they
are a rumor that we ar a paroled or exchanged
but I dont put any confidence (my spelling) in it I
hope it is soon
Gardner, Nelson

Monday, November 28, 1864
Prisner of War at Salsbery, North Carolina
too day is a warm day and we had a funarl
(funeral) count and they was a man did (died) rit
whar we was standing he got up and spread down
his blankit and laid down and did they was one
hundred and forty seven darkeys came in other
yard with us and they lay or rolin on there knees
or are in a yard pen rather (not finished)

Tuesday, November 29, 1864
Prisner of War at Salbery, North Carolina
too day has ben a warm day and the Rebels has
ben inlisting our men they was two hundred
sixty went on it we hav ben counted fest came in
another gard shot one man dead and wounded
another three other that hapened last nit about
an hour to dark it is a bout sundown all is quiet

Wednesday, November 30, 1864
Prisner of War at Salsbery, North Carolina
this day is a pleasant day and every thing goes off. well and we drad a half a loaf of bread and a peas of meat. I sold my vest to John Holin for 10 dolars and I buy bread for it that what ails me is the mater
Nelson Gardner Seventh County, Wisconsin

Thursday, December 1, 1864
Prisoner of War at Salsbery, North Carolina
well too day we draded quarter of rashans and it is hunger times hear now they was two kilt this morning over a loaf of bread they ar a gra (great) deal of talk about the exchange but I dont belav (believe) it till that day comes

Friday, December 2, 1864
Prisner of War at Salbery, North Carolina
this day is a pleasant day and we hav dra half loaf of bread hunger times hear now and it has ben so ever since we have been hear nothing going on hear today
this is from Nelson Gardner

Saturday, December 3, 1864
Prisoner of War at Salsbery, North Carolina
this morning we got up farly urly and drad a haf loaf of bread and half pint of ris soop and that wil do us for another day at least it will hav too do us nothing special too day not much too day
Nelson Gardner

Sunday, December 4, 1864
Prisner of War at Salsbery, North Carolina
sitting up by an old oak tree behind mi tent this
thing that I liv in made out of sod and a britchs
coten (britches cotton) this morning we dru a half
loaf of bread and other boys are looking for som
ris and soop but mayby they will get it and mayby
they wont. I dont no as it is you cant tell nothing
about it.

Monday, December 5, 1864
Prisoner of War at Salsbery, North Carolina
this day has ben a plesent (pleasant) day too day
we dru a loaf of bread too day and we dont had
anything for soper hunger times hear

Tuesday, December 6, 1864
Prisner of War at Salsbury, North Carolina
this day has sliped away pirty well two hundred
and fifty cam in too day and they was four
hundred and fifty in listed (enlisted) and went out
they got a loaf of bread and fifty dolars.

December 7, 1864
Prisner of War at Salsbery, North Carolina
this day has ben a dark day and it comenst too
rain this morning about two oclock too rain and
it rained till eight this morning and then cleared
up and now it is clear and the sun is clear and
everything is lively and this goes changes by

Decemer 8, 1864
Prisner of War at Salsbery, North Carolina

this day is a midlin cold day and I hav ben talking about traiding up mi coat for a Rebel coat we will haftoo (have to) go too roll call pirty quick and everything is luvly wee hav drad bread and soop too day.
Nelson Gardner
9 regiment
Wisconsin, voluntear

December 9. 1864
Prisner of War at Salesbury, North Carolina
this morning is a dark cloudy morning and it comenst raining and haling (hailing) and snowing and haling all at the sam tim that was ten oclock and it stormed all day and it is very disifreabed (?) hear now it is a tuff old storm you may bet and God nos when it is a ganto stop for I dont no our fier (fire) is por and our grub (not finished)

December 10, 1864
Prisner of War at Salsbury, North Carolina
it stormed all nit till this morning and now it has stoped and it is very slopy under foot. the snow and ise (ice) fell about three inches and now it is thawing som and I think it will turn intoo a rain in a short tim we drad meat this morning, soop and bread meat for the first time in a good whil

December 11, 1864
Prisner of War at Salsbury, North Carolina
this day is a dark old day and last nit it rained all nit long and now it has stoped and it is groing (growing) cold and the wind blas hard sno is most

all off the ground this morning. we dru some
wheat bread for the firt ime since we have been in
the confedriacy

Monday, December 12, 1864
Prisner of War at Salsbery, North Carolina
well this day is a cold day you may bet last nit the
ground froz about four inches and the fournoon it
had rained and this afternoon it coments friesion
(freezing) and it is cold you may bet the men in
this camp suffer with biter friese they ar sum
hant got any shoes nor anything else

Tuesday, December 13, 1964
Prisner of War at Salsbery, North Carolina
this day is a midlin cold day it is thawing sum
it is tuff time hear now the Rebels are in camp
recrutin how many they got I dont no but I think
they got three hundred we drad sum meat today
and sum bread and soop.

Wednesday, December 14, 1864
Prisner of War at Salsbury, North Carolina
this holy day is a mudy tim here now this camp
is more lik a hog pen then anything else. we hav
been out to a funeral count this morning we dru a
quarter of loaf of bread and they say that we are a
guntoo (going to) get another quarter too day but
I dont believe it for that is the talk every time

Thursday, December 15, 1864
Prisner of War, Salsbery North Carolina
this day is a rainy day and I have sold mi coat for
a Rebel jackit and 15 dolars

Friday, December 16, 1864
Prisner of War at Salsbery, North Carolina
this day I feal first rate and the sun shines and rains too day I traded up my Rebel pants for sum blu pants and I give fiv dollaars to boot.

Saturday, December 17, 1864
Prisner of War at Salesbery, North Carolina
today I don't feel very well I hav a pain in my bowels we are in layin in our tent Apker (Pvt. James) is cooking what litil uper (little supper) we have we dru sum meat too day and also bread rise soop.

Sunday, December 18, 1864
Prisner of War at Salesbery, North Carolina
today I feal first rate this morning we dra (drew) bread before day lit this day is cloudy it commensed raining about 12 oclock it is drislin now sum the wind is in the north and it is dark and cloudy we are out of afir (fire) wood we havent got any fir in our fir place

Monday, December 19, 1864
Prisner of War at Salesbery, North Carolina
today has been a purty fair day this morning it rained a litel and it quit again and the sun has shone most of the time but it is cloudy now the wind is in the north and it hales (hails) quite hard this morning we dru haf loaf of bread and some rise soop we are on a funderal count now and I am riting

Tuesday, December 20, 1864
Prisner of War at Salesbery, North Carolina
this morning we dru some bread that was baked
in the ground we have had a funeral count and I
flanked in another squad it dont rain today until
now it is raining some and it is cold now

Wednesday, December 21, 1864
Prisner of War at Salesbery, North Carolina
last nit it commense to raining about dark and
it rained all nit and it cleared up and now it
commens raining again it has been sloppy all day
this morning I drad a extra half loaf it is growin
cold and the wind is blowing hard and three men
are standing around the building

Thursday, December 22, 1864
Prisner of War at Salesbery, North Carolina
too day has been a cold day it stopped raining
last nit and it commense freezing and it is cold
and everything is freezen up this morning we
dru molasses in the place of meat and we dru
molasses for the first time sense we have been a
prisner

Friday, December 23, 1864
Prisner of war at Salesbery, North Carolina
this morning is purty cold the wind blew and
everything is cold it is getting warmer here
everything looks hard we dru a half loaf of bread
too a man but I dont drad any soop yet Jim
Cannon (?) is in our tent now men is suffering in
this place now but I have suff (suffered). sum you
may bet

Saturday, December 24, 1864
Prisner of War at Salesbery, North Carolina
this morning we dru potatoes and bread and ris
soop as usual the rumor is too day that we ar too
hav a loaf of bread tomorrow but I don't believe it
the weather is purty for too day what it has been
but it is midlin warm the sun got clear too day

Sunday, December 25, 1864
Prisner of War at Salesbery, North Carolina
today is Cristmas we ate our soup and bread
too day is a fogy and cold day this is the dulest
Cristmas that I ever saw but better days are
comin

Monday, December 26, 1864
Prisner of War at Salesbery, North Carolina
this day has been a cloudy time here today and
it rains once in awhile it rained all last nit purty
much we are just cooking our supper we havent
ate any time today I had a shave too day we have
drad nothing but bread and soop

Tuesday, December 27, 1864
Prisner of War at Salesbery, North Carolina
this morning we drad quarter rashens too day we
had about five hours of fair weather today we had
a funeral count I think it is hungry times hear
they was a lot of men got out last nit they tundled
(tunneled) out under the fence and they ar gone

Wednesday, December 28, 1864
Prisner of War at Salesbery, North Carolina

this moorning we dru a half loaf of bread and ris
soup it has been foggy all day last nit it rained
all nit and it is raining now God noes when it is a
ganty (going to) stop for I dont it has rained about
all the month this year is muddy and is about
knee deep and good prospect of it being deeper.

Thursday, December 29, 1864
Prisner of War at Salesbery, North Carolina
this day has been a cold day and we dru a half
loaf bread it is so dark that I cant rit

Friday, December 30, 1863
Prisner of War at Salesbery, North Carolina
this day is a cold day the wind blos hard and it is
mudy under foot this morning we dru a half loaf
of bread and half pint of ris soop and that is our
days supply there is a great talk of being paroled
but I dont believe it

Saturday, December 31. 1864
Prisner of War at Salesbery, North Carolina
this day has been a storm day it commensed
raining this morning and now it has turned into a
snow storm and it blos lik everything we dru half
loaf of bread and our ris soop it is hard tim here
and cold you may bet but got no wood and no fir
and it is colder than hel

Sunday, January 1, 1865
Prisner of war at Salsbery, North Carolina
this day is mi birthday and it is cold the ground
fross (froze) last nit bout four inches and it is cold

it is colder than I ever saw in North Carolina we drad a half loaf of bread and some bean soop and it mixt together and molasses bean soop for the first time since have had ben in this camp "Nelson Gardner born January 1, 1846—now 19 years old- el"

Monday, January 2, 1865
Prisner of war at Salesbery , North Carolina
this morning we dru a half loaf of bread we dont got our soop yet it is cold and it ant quite as cold as it was yesterday there ar strang talk of us getting out of hear

Tuesday, January 3, 1865
Prisner of war at Salesbery, North Carolina
this hav now ben a purty clair (clear) day but it has coments raining now and it looks as if it was aganta (going to) be a wet spell this morning we dru a half loaf of bread and some meat and ris soop the soop was so salt that I could hardly eat it I traid mi share for another to John Oguhn (?) I got fiv dolars too bot

Wednesday, January 4, 1865
Prisner of war at Salesbery, North Carolina
this day has been a fine day it quit raining last nit about dark and it has ben fair wether too day considering the place we had a funeral count too day this morning we dru a half loaf of bread and our soop we bot a loaf of bread for two dolars and a quart of meal for two dolars

Thursday, January 5, 1865
Prisner of War at Salesbury, North Carolina
this day has ben a purty air day this morning we dur sum meat and a half loaf of bread and soop we bot a stick of wood for a dolar we dru wheat bread too day

Friday, January 6, 1865
Prisner of War at Salesbury, North Carolina
this day has ben a wet day it coments raining about two oclock and it rained till three oclock in the afternoon and it is wet and cloudy and very mudy we dru a half loaf of bread and our soop and now mi super is ridy (ready) I bot a loaf and a half for three dolars.

Saturday, January 7, 1865
Prisner of War at Salesbury, North Carolina
this morning we dru sum turnips and half loaf of bread turnips for the first tim since we hav ben prisner last nit it rained and the wind bloed (blowed) for cris sak and it is still mudy in this prison camp we(cut Hollingshead bread for him?-not legible)

Sunday, January 8, 1865
Prisner of War at Salesbury, North Carolina
this morning we dru a half loaf of bread and soop we ar a war prisoner I hav got the shits for crist sak

Monday, January 9, 1865
Prisner of War at Salesbury, North Carolina

this morning we dru quarter rashens and our soop I feal sum beter too day the diree (diarrhea) has checked and we had a funeral count and I staid (stayed) in quarters

Tuesday, January 10, 1865
Prisner of War at Salesbury, North Carolina
this day we dru half loaf of bread and meat it comments raining about half past seven last nit and it rained till three in this afternoon and it thundered and litend (lightning) for God sak and the wind bloed (blew) and wet our tent and threw blankets and all I went out for wood and it was as wet

Wednesday, January 11, 1865
Prisner of War at Salesbury, North Carolina
this morning we dru molasses and half loaf of bread I felt sum beter too day the ground has drid up considerbal since last nit it is purty fair weather now it is purty windy we cant keep any fier (fire) in our fier place

Thursday, January 12, 1865
Prisner of War at Salesbury, North Carolina
this day I feal som beter we dru a half loaf of bread and sum soop the weather is purty fair what it has been that all today Newman Pitts has taken with the dieree (diarrhea)

Friday, January 13, 1865
Prisner of War at Salesbury, North Carolina
this day I feel sum beter of the dieree we dru sum

meat and a half loaf of bread this morning and I sold mi meat for half a dolar and bot (bought) a plug of too backar (tobacco) N.M. Pitts was taken wors too day

Saturday, January 14, 1865
Prisner of War at Salesbury, North Carolina
this day I feal very well but the insifhuns (sufferings) of hunger we dont drad nothing but a little ris water too day they have been in a ____ for the Southern Canfedersy Newman Pitts is purty sick he is out of his head all the while we drad soop too day but nothing else N. W. Pitts was tak insain last evening.

Sunday, January 15, 1865
Prisner of War at Salesbury, North Carolina
this day has ben a purty fair day we drad a half loaf of bread and sum molases and sum soop we hav faird purty well this day I took Newman Pitts too the sick call and traid (tried) to git him in the hospital but we didnt work it out N. Pitts is wors he is wors too day

Monday, January 16, 1865
Prisner of War at Salesbury, North Carolina
this day has been a plesant day we had a half loaf of bread too day and sum soop Newman Pitts died too day I think he died with the hart dieze (heart disease)

Tuesday, January 17, 1865
Prisner of War at Salsbery, North Carolina

too day we drad quarter rashens and we had a funeral count we formed around the outside of our tents and counted I bourard (borrowed) three dolars from Walter A. Pieztsch

Wednesday, January 18, 1865
Prisner of War at Salsbery, North Carolina
too day we drad a half loaf of bread and some molases and soop I had sum cakes too eat and py (pie) for the first time since I have been in hear

Thursday, January 19, 1865
Prisner of War at Salsbery, North Carolina
this day is a fogy day we drad a half loaf of bread and som ris soop our fier is poor I went for wood too day

Friday, January 20, 1865
Prisner of War at Salsbery, North Carolina
this day has been quiet we are cideing (considering) the times we drad a loaf of bread wheat at that and some potatoes and ris soop we haint had our rolcoll too day but the drumer is beating now.

Saturday, January 21, 1865
Prisner of war at Salsbery, North Carolina
this morning we drad a half loaf of bread and sum ris soop it cements raining last nit about ten oclock and it rained and sleet till about three in the afternoon it is about stop raining and the sun is coming out.

Sunday, January 22, 1865
Prisner of war at Salsbery, North Carolina
this day is a fogy day it has bin thunring all day the ice is all up the trees and it has coments raining and God nos when it will stop we drad a half loaf of bread too day and sum potatoes and jest (just) drad our soop.

Monday, January 23, 1865
Prisner of war at Salsbery, North Carolina
this day has been very mudy under foot it has ben a misty day we drad a half loaf of bread and soop

Tuesday, January 24, 1865
Nelson Gardner Prisner of war at Salsbery, North Carolina
this morning we drad a half loaf of bread and sum meat and soop

Wednesday, January 25, 1865
Prisner of war at Salsbery, North Carolina
this day we drad a half loaf of bread and sum soop we had too funeral rol calls it is very cold we have just bot a stik (bought a stick) of wood

Thursday, January 26, 1865
Prisner of war at Salsbery, North Carolina
this day is a cold day everything is fros up and the wind blows and our dhimly (chimney) smoks so that we hafta put it out and go too bed we drad a half loaf of bread and soop.

Friday, January 27, 1865
Prisner of war at Salsbery, North Carolina
this day has ben a cold day the wind houls around this camp for crist sak this day we drad a half loaf of bread and sum soop.

Saturday, January 28, 1865
Prisner of War at Salsbery, North Carolina
this day has ben sum warmer we haint got any wood too day we drad a half loaf of bread and sum potatoes and soop

Sunday, January 29, 1865
Prisner of War at Salsbery, North Carolina
this day we drad a half loaf of bread and sum soop I hav got the dieree (diarrhea) sum too day we drad a litell wood

Monday, January 30, 1865
Prisner of war at Salsbery, North Carolina
this morning we drad a half loaf of bread and soop it has been a purty day

Tuesday, January 31-1865
Prisner of War at Salsbery, North Carolina
this dad we drad a half loaf of bread and soop I traded (traded) pants it is coler than ushul (usual)

Saturday, February 4, 1865
Prisner of war at Salsbery, North Carolina
this day has been a pleasant day we drad a half loaf of bread and sum bean soop they ar ahlgin (a going) in too rol call

Sunday, February 5, 1865
Prisner of war at Salsbery, North Carolina
we dru a half loaf of bread and sum meat and beans soop the wind bloos and we cant keep our fir we hant drad any wood too day and hant likely too

Monday, February 6, 1865
Prisner of war at Salsbery, North Carolina
We dru a half loaf of bread and sum molases and bean soop

Tuesday, February 7, 1865
Prisner of war at Salsbery, North Carolina
we dru a half loaf of bread and molases and bean soop it coments storming last nit and it cep (kept) it up till too nit and it hailed and snowed and the ground is about three inches of snow and slop

Wednesday, February 8, 1865
Prisner of war at Salsbery, North Carolina
we dry a half loaf of bread and bean soop the snow has thawed purty well off of the ground it is fresen now

Thursday, February 9, 1865
Prisner of war at Salsbery, North Carolina
it is very slopy under foot and it is groing cold we drad a half loaf of bread and ris soop an molases

Friday, February 10, 1865
Prisner of war at Salsbery, North Carolina
we drad a half loaf of wheat bread and ris soop it is purty cold this day

Saturday, February 11, 1865
Prisner of war at Salsbery, North Carolina
we drad a half loaf of bread and sum molases and bean soop tis midlin fair weather.

Sunday, February 12, 1865
Prisner of war at Salsbery, North Carolina
we drad a half loaf of bread and bean soop the wind blows very bad and is midlin cold.

Monday, February 13, 1865
Prisner of war at Salsbery, North Carolina
this day we drad a half loaf of bread and bean soop I saw too yankey persons and they say that we ar a ganty (going to) git sum cloes (clothes).

Tuesday, February 14, 1865
Prisner of war at Salsbery, North Carolina
we drad a half loaf of bread and bean soop we drad sum blankets

Wednesday, February 15, 1865
Prisner of war at Salsbery, North Carolina
we drad a half loaf of wheat bread and bean soop it snowed and hald (hailed) all last nit the snow is thawing off

Thursday, February 16, 1865
Prisner of war at Salsbery, North Carolina
we drad a half loaf of bread and stinkin meat and bean soop it is nis (nice) weather overhead but it is mudy and under foot they ar tring too git men to go out to chop wood and take the code of honor

Friday, February 17, 1865
Prisner of war at Salsbery, North Carolina
I drad a half loaf of bread and sum bean soop
it has bin very mudy under foot it has coments
raining it is very dark and cloudy

Saturday, February 18, 1865
Prisner of war at Salsbery, North Carolina
I dru quarter rashens this morning and ris soop
they ar ishuing (issuing) cloes (clothes) but I dont
get any they was about five hundred prisnirs
(prisoners) and about fifty darkes I drad a blous
(blouse)

Sunday, February 19, 1865
Prisner of war, Salsbery, North Carolina
this day we drad a half loaf of bread and meat
and no soop they was a preacher in camp they
seen prisnirs that cam in yesterday went away
too day

Monday, February 20, 1865
Prisner of war, Salsbery, North Carolina
I drad a half loaf of bread and nothing too the sik
(sick) and part of the seventh division went away
last nit

Tuesday, February 21, 1865
Prisner of war, Salsbery, North Carolina
I drad a half loaf of bread and meat they about
nothing left hear today there ar a lot of prisnirs
(prisoners) out to the gat watin (waiting) for the
train

Wednesday, February 22, 1865
held prisner of war
we drad two loaves of bread and molases and meat and we left Salsbery about noon and marched seven miles and camped for the nit

Thursday, February 23, 1865
Prisner of war we hav marched about twelve miles to day it is raining lik fun we ar in the woods

Friday, February 24, 1865
Prisner of war we marched 10 miles it has rained all day and is raining now we are camped in the woods we folowed the railroad all the whil

Saturday, February 25, 1865
Prisner of war we marched about 15 miles we arrived at Greensboro at one oclock then we marched one mil in the woods and camp it has rained all day and hasnt run out too day

Sunday, February 26, 1865
Prisner of war we drad one pint of meal and then we left Greensboro about 11 oclock this four noon I am on top of the car wer reaching a endin for cris sak we ar at company station hear we go

Monday, February 27, 1865
Prisner of war we landed at Goldsboro this afternoon and then we marched about a mil in the woods and then we was purald (paroled) wer (where) we will go too nit I dont know

Tuesday, February 28, 1865
Prisner of war this day then got in our lines and got sum____
we marched 12 miles
"was paroled at N.E. Ferry, North Carolina and sent from Camp Parole, MD to Benton Barracks, MO on March 11, 1865 and arrived March 17, 1865" - el

TO ALL WHOM IT MAY CONCERN
Know ye, that Nelson Gardner a Private of
Captain Tator Company A, 19th Regiment of
Wisconsin Infry volunteers, who was enrolled on
the Twenty Fourth of December 1863
To serve three years or during the war is hereby
discharged from the service of the U. S. this
11th day of May, 1865 at Madison, Wisconsin by
reason of No 77 A.G. O. O.G.
("no objection to his being to reenlist is know to
exist")

Said Nelson Gardner was born in the State
of Wisconsin is 20 years of age, 5'4", dark
complexion, grey eyes, black hair, and by
occupation, when enrolled, a farmer.

Given at Madison, Wisconsin this Third Day of
August, 1865

G. R. Giddings
Col 16 US Infry
Musting Office.

The History of Salisbury Prison
(as described by Ed Curtis)

On a knoll in the beautifully maintained Historic Salisbury National Cemetery lies an area marked by the absence of individual tombstones. Under the grassy mantle and stately trees are the remains of some of the men who died at the Salisbury Confederate Prison. Eighteen trenches are marked with headstones and foot stones but there exists no record of the exact location where each soldier was placed. In a publication of the U.S. Government in 1868 it is reported that there were about 5,000 Union soldiers buried in the area that became the National Cemetery. In another Government Report published in 1871 the number of dead was estimated at 11,700. However, Louis A. Brown, author of *The Salisbury Confederate Prison*, stated after years of research that there could be no more than 5,000 who died at the Salisbury Confederate Prison.

Surrounding the trenches are the graves of some Union soldiers who were moved to the Cemetery after the War Between the States ended. These included fifty-seven who died at a nearby camp for "galvanized" Yankees and ninety-eight who died of communicable diseases and who were buried in a church cemetery. In 1866 a resolution of Congress ordered more Union dead to be moved from Lexington, Charlotte, Morganton, and other North Carolina locations and re-interred in Salisbury.

The United States Government assumed responsibility for the Cemetery in 1868 and the Salisbury National Cemetery was established in 1870 as a memorial to those who died at the Salisbury Confederate Prison. The wooden fence that Union General George Stoneman ordered built around the trenches in 1865 was later replaced by a stone wall that surrounds the entire original National Cemetery property of 5.97 acres. By 1876 headstones were erected to identify the graves of the known soldiers and to mark the mass graves of soldiers and civilians from Connecticut, Delaware, District of Columbia, Illinois, Indiana, Kentucky, Maine, Maryland, Massachusetts, Michigan, Minnesota, New Hampshire, New Jersey, New York, North Carolina, Ohio, Pennsylvania, Tennessee, Vermont, Virginia, West Virginia, and Wisconsin. The United States Government erected a monument to the Union dead in 1873, Maine to their dead in 1908, and Pennsylvania to their dead in 1910. In 1996 the North Carolina Division of the United Daughters of the Confederacy erected a bronze tablet on a granite base to help visitors see the location of the Prison in relation to the burial sites.

On May 20, 1861 North Carolina seceded from the Union and within weeks a site for a Confederate Military Prison was sought in the state by the Confederate Government. An empty cotton factory, soundly constructed and located near the main line railroad, was found on property in southeast Salisbury for a price of $15,000. The twenty year old building was made of brick and had three stories plus an attic. It was surrounded by a number of smaller cottages. These buildings were hastily converted for the prison compound and a wooden stockade eventually surrounded most of the sixteen acres of land. By the summer of 1862 a First National Flag of the Confederate States of America flew in front of the Prison Headquarters.

One hundred twenty prisoners of war were the first to occupy the Salisbury Prison on December 9, 1861. By May of the next year there were 1,400 men held at the Prison. Inside the wooden fence were large oak trees and wells of sweet water. Men occupied their time by the usual means of whittling, bartering, and writing, but here they also played baseball games in the spacious compound area. One prisoner wrote that the place was "more endurable than any other part of Rebeldom." Between June 1862 and October 1864 POW's were outnumbered by disloyal Confederates, Union and Confederate deserters, Confederate criminals and civilians. When the Union stopped the exchange of prisoners in August 1864 the population in the Prison began to rise. Additional recently captured soldiers and transferred prisoners from other areas increased the number held at the Salisbury Prison to 5,000 by October 1864. Ten thousand men were crowded into the stockade by November and conditions began to change dramatically.

The real misery for the prisoners at the Salisbury Confederate Prison began in the fall of 1864. The

Prison compound designed for 2,500 men was forced to handle four times that many. Due to the Union Naval blockade there was a shortage of medicine and medical supplies which resulted in terrible suffering of the prisoners and needless deaths. Throughout the South there was a shortage of food and the Prison was no exception. Eventually, all the buildings were taken over for hospital use, and the men were forced to seek shelter that cold, wet winter under the buildings, in overcrowded tents, and in burrows dug into the hard red soil. The death rate that had been only 2% before October 1864 skyrocketed to 28%.

Burials before the overcrowding had been in coffins and in separate graves. Records exist that indicate military burial services were even given. However, due to the large number of men dying daily after October 1864 a mass burial system was initiated. The bodies were collected daily and taken to the "dead house" to be counted and loaded onto a horse-drawn wagon. At 2:00 PM each day this wagon of the dead would be taken about ¼ mile to an abandoned cornfield where the men were buried. Eighteen trenches of approximately 240 feet each were eventually needed.

Escaping was a constant thought for the prisoners. Many tried in various ways but only about 300 succeeded. In November 1864 Robert Livingstone, alias Rupert Vincent and son of Dr. David Livingstone, lost his life in an ill-planned mass escape. Tunneling worked for some, but as many as 2,000 defected to the Confederacy to escape prison life. Two civilian prisoners who did escape were correspondents for the New York

"Tribune", A.D. Richardson and Junius H. Browne. After their return to New York they wrote many newspaper columns about their stay in the Salisbury Prison, and their articles helped reverse the no exchange policy.

The 2,000 citizens of the fourth largest town in North Carolina were outnumbered by the prisoners by the fall of 1864 which caused them some concern about their own safety. They were, however, not insensitive to the plight of the men in the Prison and were often seen taking food and clothing for their use. In November 1864 citizens requested CSA Secretary of War Seddon to remove at least half of those held at the Prison due to the shortage of space, food, and water. North Carolina Governor Zebulon B. Vance and the State of North Carolina after several attempts successfully got some clothing for the prisoners from the Union Government.

One citizen's humanitarianism was recorded by a number of soldiers keeping diaries while at the Prison. Mrs. Sarah Johnston, who lived just outside the main gates of the Prison, performed many acts of kindness. With the permission of the Prison Commandant and the help of the Prison Surgeon, Dr. Josephus Hall, she opened her doors to men of both armies who needed additional convalescent care. One young Union soldier, Hugh Berry, who died while in her care, was buried in her garden because she, as a mother, did not want to see him buried in an unmarked grave. Mrs. Johnston's loyalty was never questioned since her own son served in the Confederate States Navy. Today Hugh Berry's grave can be found in the Historic Salisbury National Cemetery where he was re-interred. His tombstone stands on the northwest side of the trenches.

Guard duty at the Prison was not popular. In 1861 the pay for a volunteer was $10 a month with a bounty of $11. By June 1862 the bounty had increased to $100 and guards were taken as young as 16 years of age. In July 1863 guard duty at the Prison was organized into a service known as the Home Guard with men between the ages of 18-50. During the course of the War guards came from various companies and regiments. The 4th North Carolina Senior Reserves took over most of the guarding of the Prison by the fall of 1864. Approximately 15,000 prisoners were held in Salisbury from December 9, 1861 to February 22, 1865.

There were ten commandants during the Prison's existence. Perhaps the most noted was Brigadier General Bradley T. Johnson of Maryland but Major John Henry Gee of Florida is also well known. In 1866 Major Gee was tried for war crimes in Raleigh, North Carolina and found innocent.

In February 1865 a new exchange program was finally approved. Men at the Salisbury Prison were divided into two groups in order to be exchanged. The largest group consisted of 3,729 of the more able-bodied prisoners who were marched to Greensboro, North Carolina and then taken by train to Wilmington, North Carolina to be received by Confederate Major General Robert F. Hoke. The second group, containing 1,420 of the sickest prisoners was sent to Richmond. The Prison then became a supply depot although it housed a small number of prisoners when on April 12, 1865 (3 days after Lee surrendered the Army of Northern Virginia at Appomattox) Union General George Stoneman arrived in Salisbury to free what he thought would be thousands of prisoners . The Prison was burned, the only one recorded as having been destroyed in this manner. The bricks from the buildings were later sold and are said to have been used in constructing some of the buildings on South Main Street in downtown Salisbury. A small house reportedly used by the guards outside the main entrance still stands on Bank Street, and a Confederate Government flag that once flew over the gates is now housed at the North Carolina Museum of History in Raleigh. The trenches, headstones, and monuments at the Historic Salisbury National Cemetery are additional reminders that Salisbury was once the home of a Confederate Military Prison.

Prison Life

(as described by W.O. Pietzsch)

The Baraboo Republic of Sauk County, Wisconsin wrote the following on May 30, 1895. The information came from W. O. Pietzsch. I found it a necessary fill in for Nelson S. Gardner's diary.

At the battle of Fair Oaks, VA on October 17th, 1864, at 5:00 p.m., after a hard fought battle in which the 19th Wis. Inf. took part, there were twenty-eight reported killed, twenty-three wounded and ninety-one missing. Of the missing, seventeen were known to be killed and wounded and the remainder prisoners. We went into the fight with 180 men and nine officers.

The following from Co. A were prisoners of war: Col. R. M. Strong, I. N. Bingman, O.H. Dwinnell, Peter Empser, NELSON GARDNER, Wm. Miller, N. W. Pitts, Giles Livingston, Frank Winchester, John Faller and W. O. Pietzsch, also Sgt. T. J. Johnson Co. E. We were marched in a drenching rain to Libby prison, where we were kept for eight days, we had to walk the floor all night and the next day after being captured to keep warm, as we were wet through and no dry clothes to put on.

October 28th at 10 a.m., we received our first meal, consisting of a piece of corn bread, a small piece of beef which we thought was not fit to eat, but we very soon changed our minds and found we could eat almost anything. What money we had was taken from us by the rebel authorities as they claimed we might bribe the guards with it and make our escape, but said that upon our release it would be returned to us (the boys are still waiting for it). Our rations here were about the same every day, corn bread, rice soup, and a small piece of fish or meat.

Salisbury Prison, 1864

On November 4th we were taken by rail in box cars, one hundred men in a car, with doors shut, to SALISBURY, N. C., where we arrived Nov. 6th after sundown, having been for three days boxed up worse than cattle, with no fresh, air but we got more of that at Salisbury than was good for us. The prison contained five acres of land with a tight high board fence, on the outside of which was a walk for the guard so that half of his body was above the fence and he could see what was going on inside. One rod from the fence on the inside was a small ditch called the dead line. Any one crossing it was shot without warning and the sentinel shooting received a thirty days furlough for doing the brave act. We have seen them kill our men when they were not near the dead line in order to get the furlough.

There was a four story brick tobacco warehouse inside the enclosure used for a hospital, and a log house to which the dead were carried. Every morning the dead wagon would back up to the door, two men would take eight or ten at a load, haul them out to the burial ground, dig a ditch six feet wide, two feet deep and as long as necessary and cover them up without any ceremonies whatsoever. In this manner there were buried at Salisbury prison in less than five months 5021 as brave boys in blue as ever carried a musket, out of 10,000 who had been prisoners.

Our full allowance of rations, consisted daily of one-half corn bread (corn and cobs ground together) about as large as a biscuit, one pint rice soup with less than a teaspoonful of rice in it. And no salt or other flavoring. The worms were boiled with the rice. Once in a while we received some molasses, and three times we had spoiled corn-beef and that was all the meat we saw while at Salisbury, with one exception, when MacGee (sic-Dr. John Henry Gee), the commander of the prison, came in to see us, and his dog came with him, but the dog did not get in far before the boys caught him and pulled him to pieces and those who were lucky enough to get a piece had fresh meat. I was not one of the lucky ones.

We were divided into divisions of 1,000 men, and each division into 10 squads of 100 men each, with a Sergeant in command of each squad. We were allowed a tent and a fly for one hundred men to shelter under, hardly enough for twenty-five men. In this part of the south it rained most of the time, but we only saw snow once during the winter of '64-65. The camp was muddy and to find shelter a part of the boys tunneled under the ground for a place to sleep during the rainy season. Many brave boys were buried in their dugouts, the ground being soaked with water and caving in. For fire we were allowed one stick of wood about six or seven feet long and from four to six inches thick for 100 men to cook and keep warm by. Heavy timber was in sight of the prison and we offered to go out under guard, cut the wood and bring it in on our backs, but they would not allow us to, for they might not be able to kill us off so fast. Water was just as hard to get: we were never so extravagant as to use it to wash in, we were only too glad to get what we wanted to drink. The rebel officers would come in to recruit for their army and for an inducement would offer something to eat, which if more precious than gold and silver to a starving man. I am proud to say that with death staring us in the face they only succeeded in getting a small percentage of the boys. As I think of it now I wonder if any of those who are trying to reduce or entirely cut off our pensions would have taken our places for one week for what pensions we are getting.

November 26th, 1864, after being forty-eight hours without anything to eat, we became very hungry and desperate and as the relief guard were being brought in the prisoners took their guns away, fired at the sentinels and were about to load again, but the cartridge box was empty and the attempt a failure. The boys broke up and buried the guns in an old well.

MacGee gave us five minutes to return the guns or he would open on us with grape and canister. After the five minutes were up he made his appearance again and gave us three minutes more, but the guns were not returned. The boys told him to shoot away as it was an easier way to die than to be starved to death. At last he offered a reward of seven loaves of bread to any one who would tell where the guns were, and that brought them. The man who told was taken to another prison.

Walter O. Pietzsch, died Madison, Wis.,

April 22, 1924

CHAPTER 4

- Photograph of Solomon Ashley Dwinnell
- Record of Reedsburg, Wisconsin in the War
- History of Company A. 19th Regiment
- 19th Wisconsin Prisoners-most at Salisbury, North Carolina
- New York Tribune, Wednesday, April 19, 1865

Photograph of Solomon Ashley Dwinnell

Reedsburg Free Press - August 2, 1872 (6)
RECORD OF REEDSBURG IN THE WAR
By S.A. Dwinnel
History of Company A, 19th Regiment (Chapter 1)

In December 1861, Rollin M. Strong having received a commission from Governor Randall for the purpose, resigned the office of Sheriff of the county, which he then held, and moving to Reedsburg, commenced enlisting a company, called the "Independent Rangers." They proposed to unite with an Independent Regiment which the War Department had authorized Colonel Horace T. Sanders, of Racine, to raise and get in if possible, as Company A. The "independent" nature of the movement, together with the personal popularity of the recruiting officer among the boys, soon filled the company to its maximum, 108 in number, fifty-eight of whom enlisted from this town. Rollin M. Strong was elected Captain, Henry A, Tator 1st Lieutenant, and Alex P. Ellinwood 2nd lieutenant.

They remained in this village, for preparation and drill, until Sunday, January 26, 1862, when — much to the displeasure and annnoyance of the Christian people here — they were ordered into camp at Racine, by way of Kilbourn City, WI to which place they were conveyed in sleighs by our citizens.

On the same day, at the close of services in the Congregational Church, a committee was appointed to communicate to Colonel Sanders, an expression of our deep sorrows, that the Lord's day should have been unnecessarily violated by taking the company from our midst at such a time; to which he gave us a very respectful reply, attributing the movement to his adjutant, Van Slyke.

The regiment entered Camp Utley, Racine, WI, January 27th. Company A was mustered into the United States service February 22nd. By an order from the War Department, of the day previous, abolishing all Independent Regiments, Colonel Sanders' organization was entered as the 19th Regiment of Wisconsin Infantry.

While at Racine the company was quartered near the bank of Lake Michigan, and suffered considerably from the chilling winds from that body of water.

On the 20th of April the regiment was ordered to Camp Randall, at Madison, WI to guard some 2,000 prisoners, which had then recently been captured at Fort Donelson, TN. Most of these prisoners were evidently from the poor whites of the South, rough in manners, degraded in appearance, and filthy in habits. It required the most rigid discipline to prevent their breeding a pestilence in camp. One company among them, the "Washington Artillery," was from the educated classes of New Orleans, LA and refused to associate with their fellow prisoners.

Camp Randall, being the grounds of the State Agricultural Society, was surrounded by a high and solid board fence enclosing some twenty acres. The prisoners barracks were near the fence, whilst the quarters of the 19th regiment were in the central portion of the grounds. A guard was constantly on duty on the outside of the camp, as also on the inside, between the prisoners and the quarters of our troops. No intercourse was allowed between them and the soldiers, except in the line of duty.

Upon the removal of these prisoners to Camp Douglass, Chicago, IL, Company A accompanied them as a guard. Joining their regiment as it passed through that city, June 2nd, they proceeded at once, by way of Washington, to Fortress Monroe, VA in the vicinity of which place, they remained four weeks, performing guard and picket duty.

AT NORFOLK

About the first of July, 1862, they were ordered to report to General Viele, at Norfolk, VA where, and in the vicinity of which, they remained, in the performance of garrison and out-post duty, until April 14th, 1863. This regiment performed more of this species of service, it is believed, than any other of our State troops.

Although the men sometimes complained that they were kept so long from more active service in the field, yet they performed their duties with fidelity.

Norfolk was a city of about 15,000 inhabitants, with the suburban town of Portsmouth, with a population of 10,000 and nearly all of them were in deep sympathy with the rebellion. The regimental guard which had proceeded the 19th, in those cities, was understood to have used a good supply of "rose water treatment," in dealing with the spirit of rebellion among the people, in which the commandant of the Post, General Viele, seemed to have more or less sympathy. The spirit of contempt and hatred towards the Yankee soldiers was especially manifest on the part of the females—the men not daring to give expression of their feelings towards them. And the women manifested their hostility, more by acts and sneers and grimaces, than by words.

An incident, related by Sergt. C. A. Chandler, will illustrate their manners. Having business through the city in the line of duty, one day, he saw in advance of him upon the sidewalk, three young women conversing together. As he approached them they spread themselves across the entire walk, evidently intending to crowd him off the curbstone into the street; but he marched directly along, upon the outer portion of the walk, brushing quite hard the clothing, and jostling the person, of the most impudent of the trio; where upon she snarled out some expression of contempt for Yankee soldiers.

The Sergeant stopped, and turning to the young women, told them that the soldiers had rights in that city as well as they—that it was useless to attempt to crowd them into the gutter, and it would be much better to succumb to their fate, than to resist; to which they made no reply, and he passed on his way.

The soldiers would sometimes hang out the United States flag, over the sidewalk, in front of their quarters, if for no other purpose than to see the women leave the walk and take to the street, or pass to the other side, as they approached it. At one time, upon one of the large thoroughfares, some of their number hung a flag over the walks on each side of the street, so that to pass under it or take to the street and mingle with the passing vehicles, was the only alternative. This treatment on the part of the troops restrained these acts of hostility and contempt towards them, and their rights were some outwardly respected.

Company A, with the regiment, continued efficient service at Norfolk, VA in guard and picket duty—a favorite with the law and order portion of the citizens.

ReedsburgFree Press -August 9, 1872
RECORD OF REEDSBURG IN THE WAR (7)
By S. A. Dwinnell
History of Company A, 19th Regiment
(Chapter Two)

They were commended by the Union, a newspaper, at that time published in the city, for "their exemplary conduct and quiet bearing." By their gentlemanly and quiet deportment they commanded the respect, and by their vigilance in the discharge of their duty they excited the wholesome fear of those who hated them.

New Year's day, of 1863, the Slaves became free, under the emancipation proclamation of President Lincoln. It was a high day in Norfolk. The negroes had a grand procession in commemoration of the event. A serious outbreak was feared by the excited populace. Extra guards were posted for preserving order and quelling the first symptoms of an outbreak; but none occurred. None need have been expected. It is not in man to avenge an act of merited justice done to themselves.

During the day the regiment called upon Colonel Viele, at his quarters, under whose command they had served for eight months. He made an appropriate address, and commended them in these words: "Trusted with important duties and responsibilities, you have not in one instance failed to fulfill them. Stationed among those who felt little kindness towards you, you have daily exhibited a noble forbearance. When no courtesy was shown you, you have not failed magnanimously to show pity towards the many misguided people, whom the enemy have left here unprotected, who have made petty efforts to annoy you."

General Dix, the commandant of that Department, had previously, in a letter addressed to Governor Salomon, of our State, made honorable mention of the regiment, and commended their conduct as creditable to themselves, and honorable to the commonwealth from which they came.

SIEGE OF SUFFOLK

Upon the banks of the Nansemond (River), VA, flowing to one of the inlets of the James river, and about thirty miles from Norfolk, is the little village of Suffolk. At the junction of the two Railways, it was an important strategic point, and was held by General Peck, with a force of 14,000 men. By the capture of a rebel mail, he learned of an intended surprise upon his forces, by Longstreet, one of the most able and daring of the rebel commanders. "Longstreet, Hill and Hood came rushing upon our lines," says Abbott's History, "with five divisions of the rebel army, expecting to sweep all resistance before them. They were met with solid shot, and bursting shells, and bristling steel. They had not cherished a doubt of their ability to cross the narrow Nansemond, seize the railroad in the rear of Suffolk, capture the city and its garrison, with all its vast stores, and then, after a holiday march, to occupy Portsmouth, and Norfolk."

General Peck was on the alert, obtained a few wooden gun-boats from Admiral Lee, threw up defences, and sent to Norfolk, VA for guns and troops.

On the 14th of April, 1863, the Nineteenth received orders to move to Suffolk, to reinforce the place—started by train at ten o'clock P. M.—reached the place at three o'clock A. M.—disembarked—went two mile further in a drenching rain and Egyptian darkness, to the camp of the 21st Connecticut, a large detail of whose men were out on picket, where most of our men obtained shelter in the tents of the friendly soldiers, and others were exposed to the severity of the storm until morning. They now had 600 men on duty.

At five in the evening an order was received to march to Jericho Creek, where they pitched their tents, which had now been brought forward.

One night they spent in rifle pits on the Nansemond (River)—boys had their first sight of rebs, in arms—anxious to get a shot at them.

Saturday night, April 21st, a large detail was made from Company A, under Sergeant C. A. Chandler, and one hundred and sixty from the regiment, under Lieutenant Ellinwood and another officer, to build a corduroy road, three hundred yards over a miry marsh, and a rough bridge over a creek, thirty feet in width, for the transportation of cannon, to a piece of rising ground in the marsh. This was effected on that night and the one following, the soldiers carrying much of the timber for the road from half to three fourths of a mile.

On Friday night previous, company A, with five others, had marched down the river; and gone into rifle pits, under command of Major (Alvin E.) Bovay, opposite the rebel battery at Hill's Point, on the Nansemond. The battery consisted of five splendid brass guns, four of them twelve pound Howitzers, and one twenty-five pounder. General Peck proposed to take this battery, and sent to Major Bovay for his men to join with other troops in the enterprise. Major Bovay plead that they were unfit for the dangerous expedition, having always been on guard and picket duty and never under fire, and thus obtained a countermanding order. When his men heard of this, they were fired with indignation at their commander and called him a granny, unfit for his position. They were anxious for active work, and were just ready for such a daring feat.

Other troops—two hundred in all—were detailed for the enterprise, under command of Colonel John E. Ward, of the 8th Connecticut, who crossed over in a gun-boat—landed unexpectedly—rushed up the river-bank and along a ravine—charged upon the rear of the fort, and captured men and guns without firing a shot on either side. This neat little affair has an honorable place in the history of the War, and threw a halo of military glory around the actors in it. The men of the nineteenth regiment felt deeply chagrined, not only because they were not permitted to share in the hazard and the honor of the enterprise, but also because the conduct of Major Bovay gave countenance of a false charge preferred against them of shirking duty, and grumbling, which resulted in the publication of an order of the General commanding, soon after, relieving them from duty on the line of the river defences, and ordering them into camp at Suffolk, VA—an order given, no doubt, in a moment of petulance arising from an incorrect statement of one of his staff officers, who fell out with Major Bovay.

From April 25th to April 30th, Company A, under Captain Strong, were on picket duty on the Nansemond—in rifle pits—the first thirty-six hours in the rain, without tents and without rest, except what they could get lying on the ground in their wet and chilled condition. Here they built and manned Fort Wisconsin, VA. There was a rebel battery on the opposite side of the river, about three fourths of a mile from them, between which and the river stretched a wide strip of marsh, covered with a growth of tall grass, through which the rebel sharp-shooters could crawl, concealed, to the river bank, and fire upon our men. Various unavailing efforts were made to shoot over combustible material and ignite the grass, when NELSON GARDNER and Ephraim Haines, of Reedsburg, volunteered to swim the river, which was about twenty-five rods wide at that point, and set fire to the grass. They were accepted by Captain Strong, and concealing matches in their hair and wearing their hats, leaped over the ramparts—plunged into the river—swam over unobserved by the enemy—set fire to the grass—rested a short time under the bank and returned in safety; although subject, all the way, to a shower of balls from the enemy's battery, and an enfilading fire from the rifle pits lower down the river. This dangerous feat has honorable mention in the history of the war; although the name of but one of the boys is given.

Soon after this, Company A, with about a brigade of other troops, were, for about two weeks, on a reconoissance (reconnaissance) towards the Blackwater—their rations failing—obliged to forage from the country—found a crib of corn concealed in a swamp—carried it to a rebel mill—miller refused to grind—gave him the alternative of surrendering his mill to their use, or being returned to headquarters as a prisoner—he chose the former—had two millers in Company A, Wm. Sweatland and Wm. D. Hobby—set them to grinding the corn, confiscating pigs from the woods, lived in Southern fashion, on "hog and hominy" for several days.

From May 23rd to June 17th, the regiment were at Suffolk, performing ordinary fatigue duty and drill. June 18th at Yorktown, VA, encamped outside the old fortifications until the 25th, when they were ordered to West Point, where they remained until July 8th, when they received orders to return to Yorktown.

Reedsburg Free Press -August 16, 1872
RECORD OF REEDSBURG IN THE WAR (8)
By S. A. Dwinnell
History of Company A, 19th Regiment
(Chapter Three)

AT YORKTOWN

Yorktown, VA is on the York river, 15 miles above Fortress Monroe. The stream at this point is about a mile in width, and the harbor will float the largest ships of war. It was strongly fortified during the Revolution. It was here that Lord Cornwallis surrendered his army of 7,000 men, with their munitions of war, to General Washington in October 1781, which in its results secured from Great Britain an acknowledgement of our independence as a nation.

The old fort contained an area of about twenty acres. In the early part of the war of the Rebellion the Confederacy built a new fort, enclosing the old one, and containing some forty acres.

With these and some other works, they frightened McClellan, when on his famous pick and spade expedition up the Peninsula in 1862, to spending a month in entrenching before he dared to move upon their works. Just as he got ready to do it, the enemy vanished, much to his disappointment and chagrin.

The last chapter left the 19th regiment at Yorktown. This village, of some half dozen homes, is within the fort. Two of them built on brick, bore the marks of solid shot thrown into their walls during the bombardment of our army, previous to Cornwallis' surrender.

The 19th, which occupied the fort in conjunction with several other regiments, were stationed in the northwest portion of the grounds, which had been used by the rebels as a kind of Gehenna—or a place for the burial of horses and mules.

The regiment were supplied with the Sibley tent. For the purpose of giving a better circulation of air, stakes were driven in the earth and the tents pitched upon the top of them. A large portion of these stakes, when driven touched upon the carcass of some of the buried animals, and the boys were obliged to breathe, constantly, the miasma arising from them. One of the members of Company A says that he drove stakes in the earth, and placing a board upon them, slept upon it; and that he was the only member of the company who escaped sickness at that time. Some of the men who were quartered there, climbed into mulberry trees and fastening boards in secure positions to the limbs, slept on them.

The old fort had been a perfect breeding place and refuge for rats, and the town was over-run with them. At night they held high carnival. A person walking the street could often toss them with his toe. The boys were obliged to cover up face and ears with their blankets when they slept, to save them from being bitten. The three or four wells in the place were cleaned out every day or two, taking out from them, from half a dozen to half a bushel of dead carcasses each time.

There was a fine spring outside the fort, but no permission could be obtained from General Wistar to bring water from it. Sickness began to prevail. Rations were given away to the colored people. One very old man, formerly a slave, who said he lived there in the days of the revolution and remembered those scenes well, received one hundred loaves at one time. The ranks were thinned and Hampton hospital filled up. During four weeks in which they were in camp there, four hundred out of about seven hundred were sent there, nineteen-twentieths of whom were sick with miasmatic fevers. Col. Sanders made several applications to Gen. Wistar, the commandant of the Post, for the removal of his regiment to a more healthy locality; and although there seemed to be no good reason why it should not be done, as there was no enemy within sixty miles, his applications were unheeded. Colonel Sanders finally succeeded—through his skill as a lawyer in working up a case—in obtaining an order from higher officials, for their removal to Newport News, VA, from which place one hundred and fifty more were at once ordered to Hampton, VA hospital. The few who were left outside the hospital were all partial invalids, unfit for severe fatigue duty.

It is but justice to the members of the regiment, to say that they all regarded Wistar as an unfeeling brute.

From this recital we can see that the sufferings of army life are by no means confined to the battle field, or to active service before the enemy, and that immense suffering may come to an army from the wanton disregard of the health and life of his troops by a single officer.

On the 10th of October, 1863, the regiment left Newport News on transport, for NEW BERN, N. C., at which place they landed on the 11th. This is one of the finest towns in the State, containing about five thousand inhabitants and situated at the confluence of the Neuse and Trent rivers. The rebels considered it an important position, and had strongly fortified it early in the war. It was wrested from their hands by the bravery of the Union troops under General (Ambrose E.) Burnside and Commodore Goldsborough, in February 1862.

Upon the arrival of the regiment in New Bern, Company A was assigned to out post and picket duty at

Evans' Mills on Brice's Creek, eight miles south of the city. At that place was a saw and flouring mill and a large plantation which had belonged to General Evans, of the Rebel army. The officers were quartered in the Evans mansion, and the soldiers in barracks erected for the purpose. From the west and south there was but one place of access, on account of intervening swamps, and that was across the mill-dam, and this enabled the Company to hold the position against superior numbers of the enemy.

At the time of the attack upon New Bern, NC, by the rebels, on the first of February 1864, Company A was attacked by a brigade of cavalry and a battery of artillery. They sent to New Bern for reinforcements and received three Companies of Cavalry and a twelve pound howitzer and men to work it. With this assistance they held the rebels in check three days. Captain Tator, who was in command of the out-post, and who was an efficient officer, sent out a cavalry scout several times a day, to watch the enemy and ascertain their position and what they were doing. At one time they found them building a bridge, evidently for the purpose of bringing over their artillery for an attack; but a severe shelling from the howitzer prevented their doing it. It is probable that the manifest boldness and daring of the Union troops, led the enemy to the conclusion that the force at the out-post was much superior to what it really was.

On the morning of February 3rd, Captain Tator received orders from General (John M.) Palmer, commanding at New Bern, to fall back to the city, soon after which, the rebels, guided by a Sesesh planter residing in the neighborhood, named Wood, marched around the swamps on the south, and coming in on the rear, took possession of the place. Company A was thus fortunately saved from being taken prisoners.

Upon their evacuation of the place, they burned their barracks and other property which they could not take with them. The rebels destroyed other property, and undertook to burn the Evans mansion, but the fire went out before much damage was done. The Confederates soon abandoned the position and Company A was reinstated. In rebuilding their barracks they tore down some buildings formerly used as slave cabins. In one of them was found an old rebel pay roll on which the name Wood, as a recruiting officer appeared; whereupon Lieut. Ellinwood and a small detail of men went out to his plantation and brought him in as prisoner. He was sent to New Bern, and from thence was delivered to the tender mercies of General (Benjamin) Butler, the commandant of the department at Fortress Monroe, who ordered him into confinement at the Rip Raps.

Reedsburg Free Press-August 23, 1872
REEDSBURG IN THE WAR (9)
By S. A. Dwinnell
History of Company A, 19th Regiment
(Chapter Four)

In the latter part of April, 1864, the Regiment was transferred to Yorktown, VA, where a week was spent in reorganizing the army of the James. Company A was under the command of Captain Tator. The regiment was commanded by Lieutenant Colonel Strong. It was assigned to the third brigade—under Colonel Sanders—first Division—under General Brooks—the eighteenth army corps—under General Baldy Smith—the army of the James— under General Butler. Accompanied by a few gun boats, the whole army was taken by transports, to City Point and Bermuda Hundred, where they landed May 6th, taking the rebels completely by surprise. The whole movement, up to this point, was admirably planned and executed.

From May 5th to the 9th, the army lay at Bermuda Hundred, except a portion of the troops who were engaged in digging lines of entrenchments across the peninsula, from the James (River) to Appomattox, VA, a mile or so from their confluence. On the 11th and 12th, the Nineteenth, with other troops, tore up and destroyed eight miles of the Richmond and Petersburg railroad, burning the ties and bending the rails.

On Friday, May 13th, the Nineteenth assisted in taking a line of rebel works, in front of Fort Jackson, and on the next day another line of works still nearer, where George Fosnot was wounded. These entrenchments were in the neighborhood of Drury's (Drewry's) Bluff,

VA, on the James. About four o'clock in the afternoon of Saturday, the rebels got the range of our troops and two men of the regiment were killed by shells.

On Sunday, loud cheering was heard by the Nineteenth, along the lines towards Richmond. Through rebel prisoners, afterwards taken, they learned that General (Pierre) Beauregard, with his troops from Charleston, SC had arrived, and that General R. E. Lee and Jefferson Davis were there reviewing their forces.

On Monday morning, May 16th, there was a dense fog and the rebels were early on the advance. Companies A and E, of the Nineteenth, were nearer the rebel lines than the others. Col. Strong, wishing to ascertain their position and give an order for their retreat to a position of greater safety, started out on reconnaissance . When but a short distance from his regiment, he found himself captured by four stalwart Tennesseeans. They were lost in the fog and did not know the direction of their own troops, from whom they were separated. Col. Strong at once entered into familiar conversation with them, and expressed the desire to be taken immediately within their lines, as he had been without rest for forty-eight hours and greatly needed sleep. Reposing some confidence in him as their guide, they were adroitly led in the direction of his regiment, who were lying down. When near his own men, he asked to be released from the grasp of his captors, sufficiently to take out his pocket handkerchief. The instant he was free, he bounded towards his regiment and gave the command, "attention!" in such a tone that they arose and brought their rifles upon the Tennesseeans, who cried out, "don't fire," and were soon sent to the rear as prisoners, expressing their satisfaction that they had fallen into the hands of the Union troops.

During the day the rebels pressed upon our troops and drove them at all points. During the afternoon the

Midlin Times

Nineteenth was ordered to dislodge the enemy, who was concealed in timber. To do it they were obliged to march across an open field, eighty rods, exposed all the way to a raking fire. For some reason they were not ordered to the charge upon the double quick as usual.

During the day the regiment lost thirty-two in killed and wounded. Company A lost B. S. Pitts, killed, and W. T. Reynolds, J. H. Stull, A. C. Turtle, John Fosnot, John Thorn, H. C. Feegles, and Charles Day, wounded. It was noticed that nearly all who were at this time wounded in the regiment, died, even where they suffered but slight flesh wounds, which led to the supposition that the balls of the enemy were poisoned.

The regiment was ordered to Point of Rocks, on the south of the Appomattox (River), and some ten miles from Bermuda Hundred. While there, they were out on a raid upon the Richmond and Petersburg Railroad, and tore up and destroyed some six or eight miles of the track. Some of the men were detailed to guard a baggage train sent to Grant's army at Cold Harbor.

On the 20th of June they were ordered into the trenches on the southeast of Petersburg, VA. These trenches were the advanced line of works next to the enemy. They were on duty forty-eight hours and off duty for the same length of time. They were relieved at midnight and ordered upon duty at the same hour; so they had but one night of unbroken rest in four. While upon duty, they were constantly exposed to the shells of the enemy, both night and day. During the day they suffered from sharp-shooters.

June 29th - S. Searl was killed while reading the Baraboo Republic, a ball glancing from the limb of a tree, passed into his head.

July 5th -- W. W. Holton was wounded and Ephraim Haines mortally so—the latter by a sharpshooter. About the same time, and near the same spot, a ball from the same direction passed between the legs of Sergt. C. A. Chandler.

July 13th - Corp. L. H. Cohoon wounded by a shell.

August 6th — C. A. Danforth severely wounded by a sharpshooter while eating his supper, the ball passing in at the shoulder and out through the left cheek, shattering the lower jaw.

August 7th — R. Cheek killed by a sharpshooter.

August 18th - the Veterans, two hundred and fifty in number, left on a furlough of forty days; soon after which the non-veterans were ordered to Norfolk to engage in provost general duty.

Reedsburg Free Press - August 30, 1872
REEDSBURG IN THE WAR (10)
By S. A. Dwinnell
History of Company A, 19th Regiment
(Chapter Five)

Upon the return of the veterans from their furlough, about the first of October, they were ordered to report at Chapin's Farm, on the north of the James, before Richmond, VA. On the evening of October 26th, the men of the nineteenth, with Butler's eighteenth corps, moved out from their line near Dutch Gap canal, advanced northward, and the next day, in the afternoon, formed near the old Fair Oaks battlefield, VA. They would easily have taken the defences had not the enemy learned of our movement and sent reinforcements rapidly from Petersburg. The Nineteenth regiment advanced with the other troops to assault the rebel works. Lieut. Col. Strong says: "The Regiment emerged from the pines and came out on a clear open field, about two hundred yards from the works. As we broke cover, the rebels opened on us furiously with artillery, and cut us up badly. Upon seeing the rebel works, the boys cheered lustily and advanced rapidly, closing up the breaks in the ranks made by the artillery, and preserving a splendid line. Thus for about one hundred yards, where we were met by a perfect tornado of shot, shells, canister and minnie balls directly in our faces, mowing us down by scores. The regiment was decimated—mere fragments of the line remained; dead and wounded covered the ground passed over. The few brave boys pressed forward with the same old cheer, and closed upon the colors. The order, 'lie down,' was given. Flesh and blood could go no further. Nothing could withstand the perfect blast of lead and iron—that most murderous, scourging, devouring fire. We lay down and made as thin as possible. No power to move forward or backward, or to assist in the least, our wounded comrades. The same fearful telling fire was passing over us; to raise a head was death; a hand to be hit. It was raining now, fine rain-mist and the early dark of a rainy evening was slowly enveloping us, and our earnest prayer was, 'night or Blucher,' when beyond our left a yell was heard, and the hurried tramp of men, and we were surrounded and prisoners." The Regiment numbered eight officers and one hundred and ninety men who went into the fight. Forty-four men only came back. Col. Strong was wounded by a sharp-shooter as he was making some observations to see if there was any chance for his men to get to the rear, after the order to lie down. His leg was amputated at Libby Prison (Richmond, VA).

Company A went in with thirty-six men and came out with thirteen. Corp. A. Rathbun was wounded so near the edge of the field that he was brought off on a stretcher. Sergt. E. A. Dwinnell was wounded in the head, thigh, left arm, and right hand, the latter severely, a minnie ball passing through it, and yet he backed off the field, some sixty rods, drawing his knapsack at his head, and escaped to a place of safety. Two balls in addition passed through his clothing.

Sergt. C. A. Chandler escaped from the field entirely unharmed in this manner. When he received the order to lie down, he saw a dead-furrow near him and he fell into that. The field had been sowed in wheat the summer previous, and a small growth of weeds grown up after the harvest. This furnished some protection. He raised up his head several times to look over the field and saw men attempt to run to the rear, but they uniformly fell after running a short distance.

He discovered, also, that when he raised his head, he attracted a shower of balls, and found it necessary to keep quiet. After a time he began to back down the dead-furrow, drawing his knapsack at his head for some twenty rods, when the rising ground brought him out in full view of rebel works. He then got up and run obliquely across the field, to a ditch some twenty rods distant, which he remembered to have passed over as they advanced to the charge. During all the time he was running, there was a perfect storm of bullets whistling all around him. He has no doubt that hundreds were fired at him, and yet not one touched his person, and but one his clothing. Once in the ditch he escaped without difficulty.

Edward L. Leonard was in this battle but was in a Company of sharp-shooters. They crept along a ditch to a position about twelve rods from the rebel fort, where they lay and picked off the gunners. Occasionally the Rebs would pour an ineffectual charge of grape or canister at them. There was but one of their number wounded during the action.

Wm. Miller was mortally wounded in the battle. When the prisoners were being taken from the field, he asked the rebel guard to allow one of them to remain with him and take care of him. He was answered that it could not be allowed, but that some of their own men would be along soon and take care of him, which was no doubt done, as he is reported to have died in Richmond a few days subsequently.

Sergt. F. B. Palmer, whose family resided in this village during the war, and who were highly respected, was killed during the action, but none of his comrades saw him fall. He carried the guidon on the right of his regiment and next to the 148* New York. A soldier of the latter regiment told E. A. Dwinnell that he was shot through the head. Major Vaughn escaped from the battle-field just as the rebels were charging out to secure their prisoners, and was in command of the regiment at Chapin's Farm during the winter.

On the morning of April 3rd, 1865, the Nineteenth, with their brigade, was the first to enter Richmond, and their flag was the first to float over the captured capital of the dead Confederacy. Colonel Vaughn planted it upon the City Hall. When the regiment was ordered to advance upon the works before the city, the men expected to storm them, but found them evacuated.

The non-veterans were mustered out at the close of their term of service, April 28th. The others moved from Richmond to Fredericksburg, and on May 1st were consolidated into five Companies. They were mustered out at Richmond, and August 9th, two hundred and sixty-five in number, they started for Wisconsin, where they were entertained at the fair, in Milwaukee, and were disbanded at Madison.

Reedsburg Free Press - September 6, 1872
REEDSBURG IN THE WAR (11)
By S. A. Dwinnell
Life in Rebel Prison,
at Libby, and Salisbury, N. C.
Extracts from the Diary of a member
of the 19th Regiment.
(Chapter One)

Oct. 27th, 1864.-- Near old battlefield, Fair Oaks, Virginia. Drew up in line of battle—charged out of the woods into the open field, where we were welcomed by a terrible shower of bullets from the rebel infantry, and grape and canister from their fort—our ranks were quickly thinned—some of our best and bravest men fell—still on we went nearly half a mile, until we were left alone in the open field, directly opposite the rebel fort—ordered to drop down— here we lay, hugging mother earth and praying for darkness and release—about half an hour before dark, the rebels charged out, flanked us and took us prisoners.

After a fatiguing march of seven miles, over a muddy road—it had been raining all the afternoon—we arrived at Richmond, VA at eight in the evening—were quartered in Libby prison, and laid down to rest on the bare floor.

Friday, Oct. 28th.- There are four officers: Strong, Holley, Schurff, and Wentworth, and seventy-four men here, out of two hundred and twenty of our regiment who went into the fight.—Quite a number of these are wounded. [Of these prisoners there were from Reedsburg, Col. R. M. Strong and Isaac Bingman, O. H.

Dwinnell, Peter Empser, Nelson Gardner, Wm. Miller, Walter Peitzsch, Newman Pitts, Giles Livingston and Franklin Winchester.—S. A. D.] At 10 A.M. we received our first meal, consisting of a piece of corn-bread and a small piece of beef. Soon after, we were ordered to give up all the greenbacks in our possession—knapsacks, haversacks, canteens and rubber-blankets were taken from us—most of the boys were searched. This is the manner in which this "Southern Chivalry" treats Union prisoners.—Cursed be a set of men who will rob a prisoner. At 5 P.M. our second meal was brought—bean-soup and corn-bread. We are in a large room, on the third floor of a four story building, formerly used as a tobacco warehouse, but since the war, converted into a prison—well known as Libby.

Saturday, Oct. 29th.- Pleasant. Quite a number of prisoners brought in to-day. Grant is reported to have taken the Danville Railway—if this be true, we shall probably be sent off ere long—either to some Southern prison, or back to our lines. The latter would of course be more acceptable to us. Our meals were the same as yesterday.

Sunday, Oct. 30th.- Pleasant. Last night eight of Sheridan's men—prisoners-of-war confined in the next room to us—made their escape, with four of the rebel guards. This prison, as well as the one on the opposite side of the street, is guarded by citizens, impressed for the purpose. They are without uniforms and some of them even without accoutrements. Seemingly they would rather be within our lines than here. Prisoners report that Grant has punished the enemy severely, south of Petersburg.

Monday Oct. 31st.- Pleasant. Received our rations as usual—bean-soup and corn-bread. Early in the morning sharp musketry firing was distinctly heard—a sign that our forces are not very far off. We are all praying for deliverance from this loathsome prison-life. Our fare is not sufficient to satisfy hunger. Notice of our being paroled would be hailed with exceeding joy by all.

Tuesday, Nov. 1st, 1864.— Pleasant. Our rations just sufficient to keep us from starvation. The bean-soup is full of crocodiles, and this afternoon I found the hind quarter of a rat in it. This forenoon we espied our officers in the building opposite to ours. It was somewhat amusing to see these shoulder-striped gentlemen look at us through the grates. Such is soldier life. The mud on our floor being about six inches deep, the overseer sent some darkies—prisoners like ourselves—to clean it, and now we feel more comfortable. We are all in good spirits, confident that Grant will soon be able to deliver us from our situation.

Wednesday, Nov. 2nd.- Cold and cloudy—room airy—obliged to walk the floor nearly the whole day to keep warm. The surgeon, a young, gentlemanly fellow, attends the sick once a day. About 600 Union prisoners—Sheridan's men, taken in the Shenandoah—sent South this afternoon. Our turn will probably come next.

Thursday, Nov. 3rd.— Misty and cold. About noon the Clerk went through the several rooms, taking down the number of each regiment, brigade, division and corps to which we belonged. Towards evening we received two days' rations. And such rations!—A loaf of bread, a piece of salt fish, and a piece of what they call pork in the Confederacy.

Friday, Nov. 4th.— At 3 A.M. we were marched across the James to Manchester, took the cars and started for Danville—officers sent ahead of us—road very poor—cars ran slow—this the only Railroad to Richmond from the south which the rebels now have. Our guards were mostly Germans, of the Virginia militia.

Saturday, Nov. 5th.— Rather cold. Reached Danville in the morning—changed cars—arrived at Greensboro before dark—camped near depot—remained until morning. The appearance of the country and the people indicate that the Confederacy is anything but flourishing—food and clothing very scarce—Greenbacks preferred to Southern scrip by all.

Sunday, Nov. 6th.— Pleasant. Left Greensboro at 9 A.M. and arrived at Salisbury soon after dark—received no rations to-day—obliged to sell the few trinkets we had, pocket-knives, rings, handkerchiefs, gloves, and even boots and vests found a ready sale among whites and blacks—another evidence that the Confederacy is crumbling to pieces. After entering the prisoners camp, we laid down upon the ground, as there were neither barracks nor tents for us to go into.

Monday, Nov. 7th.- Had considerable rain during the night. About 10 A.M. we received some rice soup—not enough to satisfy the appetite of a rat, much less a man. There are about 10,000 prisoners here, most of whom are in a horrible condition. The majority are without overcoats or blankets—their ghastly looks prove incontestably that the rebels are actually starving the Union prisoners. Has all feeling of humanity fled from this Southern Chivalry, that they can bear to see their fellow-men starve to death? What is our own government about? Can they not devise some means to ameliorate the condition of their unfortunate captured soldiers? About 10 P.M. we drew about half a pint of flour each.

Tuesday, Nov. 8th.— A dark, rainy day. The camp is in a horrible state—no policing done—we who have no shelter are obliged to lay down in the mud. A large number of the dead are carried off every morning—stripped of every article of clothing which might be fit to be worn by some traitorous scoundrel. These Rebs taking splendid care of prisoners indeed! At night several of us managed to pitch shelter tents; so we were not exposed to the drenching rain during the night.

Wednesday, Nov. 9th.— Now since the election is over, we hope Old Abe and Butler will turn their attention to the humane and Christian-like business work of arranging for an exchange of prisoners. Our guards are North Carolina farmers, old and young, conscripted for that purpose. Our rations consisted of rice soup in the forenoon, and a pint of meal in the afternoon. At noon, tents were issued to our division; we received two—an A tent and one fly, to one hundred men. Considerable rain during the night.

Thursday, Nov. 10th.— Camp very muddy, but drying fast. One half loaf of corn bread in the morning and a cup of rice-soup, without salt, composed our rations for this day. Our life is very dull and tedious. Reading matter not to be had—no letters from home to cheer us—everything looks gloomy. I hope, in God, we will be delivered from this prison life ere long—it is killing indeed.

Friday, Nov. 11th.-- Cold and clear. Received a piece of beef in the morning—something what they call rice-soup in this country at noon, and a half a pint of corn meal in the afternoon. Now if any man cannot live on what the Confederacy so bounteously issues to him, surely has no business to be a soldier. I believe I am growing fat on Southern fare. A teaspoonful of salt was also issued to each man—another proof that Southern Chivalry feeds their prisoners sumptuously. Surely such a kind and generous people ought to be prosperous.

(Note.— Salisbury military prison was in the form of a triangle, surrounded by a fence, made of posts twelve feet high, set in the ground close together. It contained seven acres. Within the enclosure was a four story brick building one hundred feet by forty, which had been used as a cotton factory, and several small brick tenement houses which were now used as hospitals. Twelve feet from the fence, on the inside, was a ditch called the dead line. Any prisoner who should cross that line was shot by the guards who walked on a platform built near the top of the fence. The bread spoken of, was corn bread, unless wheat is mentioned—a half loaf equaled a pint of meal. It was made of corm and cobs ground together. The cup mentioned was less than a pint. The rice-soup was so poor that only three or four grains of rice were stewed to a cup full. The meat consisted usually of a small piece of liver, heart or lights—not beef or other solid meat.)

Reedsburg Free Press - September 13, 1872
REEDSBURG IN THE WAR (12)
By S. A. Dwinnell
Life in Rebel Prison, at Salisbury, N. C. Extracts from the Diary of a member of the 19th Regiment.
(Chapter Two)

Nov. 12, 1864.-- Night cold—day very blustering—every one at work banking up the canvass huts with mud— which article is more plentiful in this camp than anything else. Water is very scarce—the three or four wells on the grounds are either dry or so near it that the water is not drinkable—have to bring the water for cooking purposes, from outside, in barrels—wood also has to be brought in by the boys, on their shoulders, split with Railroad spikes, cut with jack-knives and broken with the hands—they have things real handy in this Corn-federacy—half a loaf of corn-bread in the morning—two spoonsful of rice at noon. Whenever we get out of this we will be able to measure the fat on our ribs —not by inches, but by rods. If this is not gay and festive, I have an erroneous idea of those two words.

Sunday, Nov. 13th.- Clear and cold. A half loaf of bread, rice soup, and a piece of beef. Many rumors are afloat about an exchange of prisoners. Seemingly the rebel papers harbor the idea that a general exchange will take place—to commence on the 15th inst.

Monday, Nov. 14th.-- Clear and cold. A half loaf of bread and a cup of rice-soup . I believe I could eat this kind of food a whole year and not get fat on it—at least, so far, I have not gained much. Lincoln is doubtless elected President of the United States by a large majority. During the next four years, I hope he will be able to restore the Union in all its integrity. The sufferings of the prisoners are severe indeed, especially during the cold nights—many being without coats or blankets, are compelled to spend the nights in walking over the camp-grounds. The wood furnished us is scarcely sufficient to cook our scanty rations—much less to keep ourselves warm. Should we have to remain here during the coming winter, many of us, I fear, will freeze to death. So much for Chivalry!

Tuesday, Nov. 15th.- Cloudy and cool. The Salisbury Watchman contains the news that Lincoln has called out a million of men to suppress the rebellion. Rations as usual—gay living this.

Wednesday, Nov. 16th.-- Cold and cloudy. A half loaf of bread and a cup of soup. Time passes very slowly. No newspapers or other reading matter to be had—no letters from home to make our loathsome life agreeable—no letters can be sent to our friends in the north. It is hard to be stripped of everything which makes life pleasant, and then, in addition, to endure the process of slow starvation, to which we are subjected. It is enough to make us swear eternal vengeance on the instigators of all this misery. But despair not! Trust in Him who doeth all things well!

Thursday, Nov. 17th.- My brother's birthday. He too is far away from everything dear to him, exposed to death in the holy work of suppressing this wicked rebellion. Let us hope to meet when the war terminates and peace comes again. One-half loaf of bread and a cup of soup—ought to have had meat today, but did not get it—perhaps they fear we will break out of this camp if they feed us too highly. Several trains loaded with exchanged Rebel soldiers, passed here on their way south.

Friday, Nov. 18th.— A beautiful day. Rations—half loaf of bread and a cup of soup. Our tent was raided upon at 11 P.M., by a number of thieving scamps—prisoners like ourselves—and two overcoats and one blanket were taken. Stealing is the order of the night here, and those who are so fortunate as to possess these articles, have to watch them closely.

Saturday, Nov. 19th.- Rainy and cold. Corn-meal and a cup of soup—the meal was the poorest I ever saw—cobs and husks seemed to have been ground with the corn—however it is good enough for Yankee prisoners. We eat it because hunger compels us to do so. Oh! For this magnanimous and kind-hearted chivalry! Surely Savages cannot abuse prisoners-of-war any worse than this confederacy does us.

Sunday, Nov. 20th.- Rain. What a Sabbath! What a contrast between Wisconsin and North Carolina! Surrounded by misery, destitution and death, we are called upon to offer up our prayers to the Almighty. Prayers uttered in a place like this must be heard by the Spirit above; it cannot be otherwise. Thousands are praying to be delivered out of the hands of a miserable set of human beings who profess to be Christians. "Feed the hungry and clothe the naked" is certainly not contained in their bible. Let us hope that He will, ere long, free us from the yoke so burdensome to us. Rations the same as usual.

Monday, Nov. 21st.— It still rains. The Camp is in a horrible condition. A cup of soup and a pint of corn-meal. From October 3d to yesterday, 1,127 Union prisoners have died in this yard. We are sitting in our tents shivering with the cold.

Tuesday, Nov. 22nd.- Cloudy and cold. Bread and soup as usual. Impossible to describe the sufferings of the prisoners—must be seen to be realized.

Wednesday, Nov. 23rd.— Clear and cold. Last night was the coldest I have experienced in Dixie. A number of men froze to death; and this is in the year of our Lord, one thousand eight hundred and sixty-four! What will be the punishment of these traitors who have caused all this misery? Will they be allowed to disgrace the halls of Congress again with their presence? Hanging is too light a punishment for these scoundrels. Bread and soup as usual.

Thursday, Nov. 24th.-- Night cold, day pleasant. This being Thanksgiving-day, the Rebel Authorities thought to let us know it; and they did it effectually by issuing only a quarter of a loaf of bread and a reduced ration of soup. Just think of it! Four ounces of corn-bread and less than a pint of thin rice-soup to a man for a day. This is being killed by inches. Is there no humanity about these traitors? Seemingly not. But then, men who will perjure themselves before their God are also capable of killing their fellows by the slow process of starvation. And our own Government—will they not awake to the duty of liberating us from the clutches of Rebel demons? Will not the Almighty inspire the Union Authorities, that they may endeavor to effect our exchange? And thus save the lives of thousands of unfortunate beings who have exchanged the comforts of home—have risked their lives on battlefields, and suffered all the trials and dangers of Soldiers life, that the nation might be saved from a traitorous foe.

Friday, Nov. 25th.— Pleasant day. Rations—quarter loaf of corn-bread, small piece of meat and rice-soup. About 2 o'clock P.M., an effort was made, by a number of prisoners, to break out; about twenty of the guard were knocked down and their guns taken from them. There being no organization throughout the camp, the affair was an entire failure and was easily suppressed. A number of innocent men were killed and wounded, and nothing was accomplished.

Saturday, Nov. 26th.— Pleasant. Four ounces of bread and a cup of rice-soup, with little rice in it, and no salt. Being well aware of the starving conditions we are in, recruiting officers make their appearance in camp frequently, to enlist men for the rebel ranks. And there are men—I am ashamed to say it—in this camp, vile enough to commit perjury, and join the ranks of traitors. Starvation is their excuse for doing it. For my part I would rather be carried out of Camp on the dead-cart than to have the brand of traitor upon me. I shall be patient, trusting in God till the tide of events shall take me back under the folds of the glorious stars and stripes, that I may again raise my shout and my sword —For God and Liberty—For Justice and Truth. Join a traitorous foe! No! Never!

Sunday, Nov. 27th.- Cloudy. Some rain. Something must have happened to the Confederacy; we received a half loaf of bread, a piece of meat and a cup of rice-soup—the best we have had yet. It is rumored that Sherman has taken Milledgeville, Georgia.

Monday, Nov. 28th,-Pleasant. Four ounces of bread, meat and soup. A general roll-call this afternoon. At night a man was shot dead and another wounded, close by our tent, for loitering about the bakery.

Tuesday, Nov. 29th.— A beautiful day. A half loaf of bread and rice-soup.

In the afternoon, a recruiting officer raised 365 men for the rebel ranks, out of the prisoners confined here. Starvation and lack of clothing their excuse. What a life this is! This morning we stay in our tents until the call "Tenth Division for Bread" issues forth from the cook-houses. The prisoners are divided into Divisions of a thousand each, and these are sub-divided into squads of a hundred each. The Divisions are in charge of a Sergeant-Major—the squads under a First Sergeant. When the bread is issued, we buy a cup of water and make dope out of it, as it is not sufficiently baked to be digestible. I say we buy our water. This is essentially so. The four or five wells in camp are nearly dry, and so deep that a man who is not fortunate enough to possess a rope, is obliged to pay some tobacco, bread, thread or buttons, for his water. Our morning meal being taken, we walk up and down Broadway—an open space in the centre of the camp—hear the thousand and one bulletins that are daily circulated—go to the hospital and witness the most heartrending suffering and misery that can be imagined to exist—or witness the purchases, sales and trades at the "meat market," near the hospital. Here is where the thieves and scoundrels show their rascality. A. comes along with a piece of bread in his hand—B. snatches it from him and starts on a run. If A. is able to catch B., a knock-down usually ensues, and A. may get his bread back; if otherwise, B. can be seen going to some other part of the camp, offering bread for sale.

—Sometime in the afternoon, when soup is issued, we devour it with the remainder of our bread. Do our every-day "skirmishing after gray-backs," and take another walk on Broadway. At dark we lie down—not to rest, for that is impossible—but to while away the long, dreary hours of night in thinking of home, with its many comforts, or of our fellow soldiers, who are fortunate enough to be still under the "Stars and Stripes." When will we be released?

(Note.—On the 25th of November, a regiment of North Carolina troops, consisting mostly of haughty and reckless youth, were relieved from guard duty at Salisbury, to be sent elsewhere at night, and their places supplied by North Carolina farmers, who were known to the prisoners to be mostly Union men. A plan was laid, somewhat extensively, to make an effort to overpower the guard, at the time the relief came upon duty, on the morning of November 26th. Some reckless prisoners, hearing of the plan, could not wait, but commenced a premature attack on the previous afternoon. The firing upon the prisoners was done by the young sprigs of Southern "Chivalry," who had just been released from duty, and had not yet been sent away. They jumped upon the platform and fired upon the prisoners for some time, without restraint.

A. D. Richardson in "Field, Dungeon and Escape," says of this tragedy: "While we were sitting at dinner, John Lovel came and whispered to me, 'there is to be an insurrection. The prisoners are preparing to break out.' We had heard such reports so frequently as to lose all faith in them; but this was true. Without deliberation or concert of action, upon the impulse of the movement, a portion of the prisoners acted. Suffering greatly from hunger, many having received no food for forty-eight hours, they said 'Let us break out of this horrible place. We may just as well die upon the guns of the guards as by slow starvation.' A number, armed with clubs, sprang upon a rebel relief of sixteen men, just entering the yard. Although weak and emaciated, those prisoners performed their work promptly and gallantly. Man for man they wrenched the guns from the soldiers,— one rebel resisted and was bayoneted where he stood. Another raised his musket, but before he could fire, fell to the ground, shot through the head. Every gun was taken from the terrified relief, who immediately ran back to their camp outside. The insurrection—which had not occupied more than 8 minutes—was a failure, and the uninjured returned to their quarters. The yard was now perfectly quiet; yet the guards stood upon the fence for twenty minutes, with deliberate aim firing in to the tents, upon helpless and innocent men. Sixteen prisoners were killed and sixty wounded, of whom not one in ten had participated in the outbreak; while most were ignorant of it until they heard the guns. After this massacre, cold-blooded murders, by the guards were very frequent.")

Reedsburg Free Press - September 20, 1872
REEDSBURG IN THE WAR (13)
By S. A. Dwinnell
Life in Rebel Prison, at Salisbury, N. C.
Extracts from the Diary of a member of the 19th Regiment.
(Chapter Three)

Wednesday, Nov. 30th — Warm and pleasant. A half loaf of bread, meat and soup. The men are dying off quite fast. From thirty to fifty victims of starvation are carried off every day, and not a friend to pay their last respects to them. The falling of a chimney in one of the hospitals, crushed to death a number of the sick, and injured many others.

Thursday, Dec. 1st — Pleasant. Quarter of a loaf of bread and rice-soup. They have an improvement on bread this morning; formerly it was made of corn-meal and wheat-flour; now it is made of the poorest of meal (com and cobs ground very coarsely) shorts and cane seed.

Friday, Dec. 2nd — Cloudy and warm. Half loaf of bread, meat and rice-soup. There is a sutler in this camp who sells things remarkably cheap—meal $1.50 a pint, flour or rice $2.00 a pint, salt $3.00 a pint, Southern pies (made of sweet potatoes) $2.50 each, and other articles in proportion. Since the riot, the rebels seem to be very much frightened — at dark all fires are ordered to be extinguished, and all the men sent to their tents. We have no guards inside of camp, and those outside are more vigilant than usual.

Saturday, Dec. 3rd — Cloudy and warm. Camp duller than usual.

Sunday, Dec. 4th — Clear and chilly. Half loaf of bread and rice-soup. Some divisions drew potatoes, but there was not enough to go around, so our tenth division came out minus.

Monday Dec. 5th — Pleasant. A half loaf of bread and a cup of soup. The clemency of the weather is a great blessing to us. Our sufferings would be intense should snow cover the ground. Our poor and scanty rations infuse but little warmth into our systems. But with God's help, we will live through it and see better days.

Tuesday, Dec. 6th — Cool. About 250 Union prisoners arrived here from Richmond, mostly captured near Point of Rocks, on the 17th ult. 437 more prisoners enlisted in the rebel ranks. What is going to happen? A half loaf of bread, a cup of soup and a half dozen potatoes—such as we up north feed our pigs on—composed our rations, and some Divisions even drew molasses.— The Corn-ederacy—or Branfederacy rather—is getting up in the world, surely.

Wednesday, Dec. 7th — Rainy during the night and forenoon. A half loaf of bran-bread and a cup of soup.

Thursday, Dec. 8th.-- Clear and cold. Bread and soup, the same as yesterday. No more.

Friday, Dec. 9th — A half loaf of wheat bread and rice-soup.

Saturday, Dec. 10th.-- Rainy and cold, night very cold. Four ounces of bread, an ounce of poor meat and rice-soup.

Sunday, Dec. 11th — Very cold. Snow covers the ground. The sufferings of the prisoners is indescribable—the dead-cart at work all the day, carrying off the victims of starvation. A half loaf of bread and rice-soup.

Monday, Dec. 12th — Cloudy and cold. Camp very muddy. Bread and soup as usual.

Tuesday, Dec. 13th — Cloudy and cold. Four ounces of wheat bread, meat and soup—275 prisoners enlisted in the Rebel army. Papers are not allowed to enter the camp, and therefore we know nothing of the military situation.

[Wednesday, Dec. 14th — Nothing recorded.]

Thursday, Dec. 15th — Cloudy and more moderate. A half loaf of bread, meat and soup. Moved our tent to a warmer place.

Friday, Dec. 16th — Cloudy. Our present life is dull in the extreme. The Camp-ground is too muddy for walking, and we are obliged to spend our time in our tents. A few prisoners brought in, report the 2d and 5th army corps to be on an extensive raid in North Carolina. A half loaf of bread and a cup of soup.

Saturday, Dec. 17th — Pleasant. A half loaf of bread, meat and soup.

Sunday, Dec. 18th.-- Misty but not cold. Bread and soup as usual. Three citizen-prisoners, Junius H. Browne, reporter of the N. Y. Tribune, A. D. Richardson, of the Tribune, and Wm. E. Davis, of the Cincinnati Gazette, made their escape.

Monday, Dec. 19th — Pleasant—& a shower at dark. A half loaf of bread and soup.

Tuesday, Dec. 20th — Cloudy and cold. A half loaf of bread and soup.

Wednesday, Dec. 21st — A heavy shower during last night. Considerable water in our tent, the air chilly, consequently much suffering. Bread, soup and three spoonsful of molasses.

Thursday, Dec. 22nd — Very cold. Bread and soup as usual. From sixty to seventy men are dying daily. At this rate it will take about three and a half months to put all the prisoners in camp under the sod.

Friday, December 23rd — Cold and cloudy. Bread and soup as usual. Quite a number of the 19th down sick—not well myself.

Saturday, Dec. 24th — Clear and pleasant. Bread and soup and potatoes. Some sixteen prisoners of Stoneman's men taken in West Virginia, brought into camp—had to march all the way—about two hundred and fifty miles— because there was no transportation for them.

Sunday, Dec. 25th — Merry Christmas we hear from every quarter this morning; but how can we be merry? Will this, our misery, never cease? Shall we be left here to die, victims of starvation? That the Rebel Government proposes to starve us is no secret; but that our own Government should bear witness to this kind of treatment and not try their utmost to ameliorate our misery, is certainly a fact that they—to say the least—ought to be ashamed of. Bread and soup as usual.

Monday, Dec. 26th — Cloudy and misty. Bread and soup. At night fourteen prisoners escaped through a tunnel. About two hundred Catholics left Camp today—going to more comfortable quarters—through the efforts of the Priest of Salisbury, who holds mass in camp nearly every day.

Tuesday, Dec. 27th — Misty and very unpleasant. A quarter of a loaf of corn bread and a cup of soup. A heavy rain during the night.

Wednesday, Dec. 28th — Misty and unpleasant. A half loaf of bread and a cup of soup. The inclemency of the weather confines us to out tents—nothing but the cold damp ground to sit on, and so crowded that our tents hardly cover us all, unless we lie down "spoon-fashion." This Confederacy is a gay concern in whatever light you look at it. Think I shall join it—over the left.

Thursday, Dec. 29th — Clear but cold. A half loaf of bread and a cup of soup. Incessant rain for the last week or two—Camp gloomy—mud knee deep—the men go about shivering with the cold—their clothes torn and tattered, and their ghastly looks and thin, pale faces, indicate the progress the slow starvation process is making. May the originators of this rebellion, and the authors of all this misery, be cursed forever by all human beings. Most assuredly the blessing of God cannot rest upon them.

Friday, Dec. 30th — Chilly and cloudy as usual. Fixing up for another storm. Glorious country this! Have not had a pleasant day in a dog's age. Everything corresponds with everything else in this Confederacy. Weather disagreeable—grub not palatable—old dead-cart gets stuck at every trip—the old codgers on the fence look as if they would rather be with the old lady at home, than here guarding Yankees. Sweet looking birds they are, with a homemade quilt around them, and the gun on their shoulders. Pretty good fellows they are, however, notwithstanding their grotesque appearance. They are very quiet, and talk with the prisoners in their quaint, homespun, ignorant style—their heads not bothered with too much knowledge, or their stomachs with too much nutritious food. Their rations poor and scanty. A half loaf of bread and a cup of soup as usual.

Saturday, Dec. 31st — Rain during the night and a foggy, chilly day. A half loaf of bread and soup as usual.

(Note.—A. D. Richardson, in "Field Dungeon and Escape" says of the Salisbury prison: "Nearly ten thousand prisoners of war, half naked and without shelter, were crowded within its narrow limits, which could not reasonably accommodate more than six hundred. It was converted into a scene of suffering and death which no pen can adequately describe. We had never been in a prison containing private soldiers, and had been skeptical as to the barbarities they were said to suffer. We could not believe that men, bearing the American name, would be guilty of such atrocities. Now it seemed to me hardly possible to exaggerate the incredible cruelty of the rebel authorities.

When captured, the prisoners were robbed of the greater part of their clothing. When they reached Salisbury, all were thinly clad, thousands were barefooted, not one in twenty had overcoats or blankets, and many hundreds were without coats or blouses.

For several weeks they were furnished with no shelter whatever. Afterwards one Sibley tent and one A tent were issued to each hundred men. With the closest crowding, they contained about one half of them. The rest burrowed in the earth, crept under buildings, or dragged out the nights in the open air, upon the muddy, snowy, or frozen ground.

They were organized into divisions of one thousand each, and subdivided into squads of one hundred. Almost daily one or more divisions were without food for twenty-four hours. Several times some of them received no rations for forty-eight hours. The few who had money, paid from five to twenty dollars for a loaf of bread.

On wet days the mud was very deep, and the shoeless wretches wandered pitilessly through it, seeking vainly for cover and warmth. Two hundred Negro prisoners were almost naked, and could find no shelter whatever but by burrowing in the earth. The authorities treated them with unusual rigor, and the guards murdered them with impunity.

No Song, no athletic games, few sounds of laughter broke the silence of the garrison.")

Reedsberg Free Press - September 27, 1872
REEDSBURG IN THE WAR (14)
By S. A. Dwinnell
Life in Rebel Prison, at Salisbury, N. C.
Extracts from the Diary of a member
of the 19th Regiment
(Chapter Four)

1865. In God we trust.

Sunday, January 1st — Clear and cold. Taking a retrospect of the military proceedings of the past year, we find much to encourage. Although, through the imbecility of two political Generals, the golden opportunity of striking the death blow to the rebellion was lost, yet we have torn a large tract of territory from the grasp of the traitors, and have, by the destruction of their supplies and crops, brought hunger and starvation upon them. Although we have suffered reverses in several instances, yet we find more than an offset for these failures, in the progress of Sherman's army—in the gallant conduct of Sherman's troops—and in the siege-operations of Grant at Petersburg. Rebellion is uttering its death groans; and taking in view the gigantic efforts of our government for its overthrow, we can but hope that before this year closes, the Southern Confederacy will be among the things that were. For myself I have much to be thankful for. A tedious illness confined me to the hospital for several weeks; yet, with God's help, I recovered and enjoyed perfect health. Having encountered a storm of deadly bullets several times, I lived through them uninjured; and although I have had the misfortune of falling into worse than savage hands, I am still alive, hopeful of again living under the stars and stripes after our release from prison. A half loaf of corn-bread, a cup of rice-bean soup and three spoonsful of molasses.

Monday, Jan. 2nd — Chilly and clear. A half loaf of corn-bread and a cup of soup. The Salisbury Watchman states that the exchange of prisoners would soon be resumed on the James river. Hope our turn will come soon.

Tuesday, Jan. 3rd — Cloudy and chilly. A half loaf of wheat-bread, a cup of soup and a small piece of salt beef. Camp drying up nicely.

Wednesday, Jan 4th — Chilly and clear. A half loaf of corn-bread and a cup of soup. Camp drying up.

Thursday, Jan 5th — Chilly and clear. Wheat-bread, soup and salt beef. A heavy rain-storm at night.

Friday, Jan. 6th — Rainy and cold. A half loaf of bread and soup.

Saturday, Jan. 7th — Clear and very windy. Bread, soup and turnips.

Sunday, Jan. 8th — Clear and chilly. Bread and soup.

Monday, Jan. 9th — Clear and cold. Bread and soup as usual. Rain at night. Private Wm. Goodnough died.

Tuesday, Jan. 10th — A very rainy day. Since 6 o'clock last night the rain has poured down steadily. Our tent full of water and our situation anything but comfortable. Still we are of good cheer, as the news reaches us that we will soon be exchanged. The happiest day of my life shall be when I return under the folds of our own starry banner. God speed the day! A half loaf of bread, a cup of soup and fresh beef.

Wednesday, Jan. 11th — Clear and windy. A half loaf of corn-bread, rice-soup and molasses.

Thursday, Jan. 12th — Clear and pleasant. With the poet we may exclaim, "Thank God for pleasant weather." The Watchman states that the Commissioners of Exchange had met at Richmond and made arrangements for an immediate exchange of prisoners, and that we would soon be taken away from here. The Lord has heard our prayers at last, and to Him will we sing praise. Bread and soup.

Friday, Jan. 13th — Smoky and pleasant. Wheat-bread, soup and salt beef.

Saturday, Jan. 14th — Clear and chilly. One pint of poor rice-soup composed our rations for this day. Reason— no flour or meal on hand. Oh! Thou glorious Confederacy. Surely thou hast merited better treatment at the hands of the Yankees because thou shewest magnanimity and benevolence towards those whom the fortunes of war cast into thy hands! Go on thy way rejoicing, thou great Rebel Chieftain; but keep away from thy persecutors, for they may ornament some tree with thy body. Ornament? No! even a tree would wither and die, should the body be suspended from one of its limbs, for thy presence is death. In the afternoon a Rebel Recruiting officer appeared in Camp, and although everyone was hungry, he had not as many customers as usual. Only about ninety committed perjury, and enlisted in the Rebel ranks. I feel quite sick to-day—head aches terribly.

Sunday, Jan. 15th — Clear and pleasant. A half loaf of bread, rice-soup and three spoonful of the poorest molasses I ever tasted.

Monday, Jan. 16th — Clear and pleasant. A half loaf of bread and rice-soup. Newman W. Pitts, one of our best boys, died this forenoon. Peace to his ashes.

Tuesday, Jan. 17th — Pleasant. A quarter of a loaf of bread and a cup of soup. News comes that Fort Fisher has been taken by our forces. How are ye Rebellion?

Wednesday, Jan. 18th — Pleasant. Bread, molasses and soup. Joh. B. Conger, Co. D died at 7:30 P.M., at Ward No. 7.

Thursday, Jan. 19th — A raw, cloudy day. John Witting, Co. C, died this morning at 3 o'clock. Bread and soup as usual. Maj. Gee, the Commandant of this Camp, told us this afternoon, that he had received tidings from Commissioner Ould, that we would be exchanged within a month. Good, if true.

Friday, Jan. 20th — Smoky and pleasant. Wheat bread, rice-soup and molasses.

Saturday, Jan. 21st — Rained all night and all day. Bread and soup.

Sunday, Jan. 22nd — Cloudy and unpleasant. Bread, soup and potatoes.

Monday, Jan. 23rd — Misty and dark. Bread and soup. These dark, gloomy days pass by very slowly; we stay in our under-ground dwellings, eat our scanty rations, and lay down on our soft beds, made of pine shavings.— Were it not for the hope of a speedy exchange, surely we would wish ourselves under the sod.

Tuesday, Jan. 24th — Clear and pleasant. John Kottinger, Co. C, died this morning. He leaves a young wife to mourn. Bread, soup and salt beef.

Wednesday, Jan. 25th — Clear and cold. Bread and soup. General roll-call in the afternoon. The Yankees are rather beating the Rebs on the ration business, and for this reason guards were placed around those who had been counted; but to no avail; the Yankees run the guards, and flanked as much as ever. The only way to stop flanking, is to give us enough to eat. As long as we are on less than half rations, we will have flankers.

Thursday, Jan. 26th — Clear and cold. Bread, soup and salt beef.

Friday, Jan. 27th — Clear and cold. Bread, soup and salt beef.

Saturday, Jan. 28th — Coldest night of the season. Day clear and cold. Bread and soup.

Sunday, Jan. 29th — Clear and cool. Bread, soup and a few frozen potatoes. Our wood allowance—slim enough for the last week—was discontinued entirely to-day. We were obliged to turn in and cover up, to keep our extremities from freezing. Go it Jeff.! (Jefferson Davis). If starvation is too slow a process to kill us off, freeze us to death. Wm. Matthewson, Co. H, died this morning.

Monday, Jan. 30th — Clear and pleasant. Bread and soup.

Tuesday, Jan. 31st — Pleasant. Bread and soup. Nearly all the able-bodied negro-prisoners taken out to-day, to work, it is said, on some fortifications, in South Carolina. No wood—could not cook dope—had to eat our bread dry.

Wednesday, Feb. 1st — Beautiful day. A quarter of a loaf of corn-bread and soup. Meat entirely played out.

Thursday, Feb. 2nd — Pleasant. Corn-bread and soup. No wood; had to eat dry bread.

Friday, Feb. 3rd — Rainy and cold. Corn-bread, soup and some poor molasses.

Saturday, Feb. 4th — Foggy morning, day beautiful. Bread and bean-soup. A Rebel came into Camp to buy

United States currency, offering $1,300 for $100. The Salisbury authorities must consider their case about played. Do you smell a mice, Mr. Reb?

Sunday, Feb. 5th — Clear and windy. Bread, fresh-beef and bean-soup.

Monday, Feb. 6th.- Cloudy and chilly. Bread, bean-soup and molasses. No wood.

Tuesday, Feb. 7th — Rainy. Bread, soup and molasses.

Wednesday, Feb. 8th — Clearing off. Corn-bread and bean-soup, without the beans.

Thursday, Feb. 9th — Clear and cold. Bread, rice-soup and burned molasses.

Friday, Feb. 10th — Clear and cool. Wheat bread and rice-soup.

Saturday, Feb. 11th — Pleasant. Bread, molasses, vinegar and bean-soup.

(Note.—A. D. Richardson, in "Field Dungeon and Escape" says: "That section of country (around Salisbury) is densely wooded. The cars brought fuel to the doors of our prison. If the Rebels were short of tents, they might easily have paroled two or three hundred prisoners to go out and cut logs, with which, in a single week, barracks could have been constructed for every captive. But the commandant would not consent. He did not furnish half the needed fuel.

Cold.and hunger began to tell fearfully upon the robust young men, fresh from the field, who crowded the prison. Sickness was very prevalent and very fatal. It invariably appeared in the form of pneumonia, catarrh, diarrhoea or dysentery; but was directly traceable to freezing and starvation. Therefore the medicines were of little avail. The weakened men were powerless to resist disease, and they were carried to the dead-house in appalling numbers.")

Reedsburg Free Press - October 11, 1872
RECORD OF REEDSBURG IN THE WAR (15)
By S. A. Dwinnell
Life in Rebel Prison, at Salisbury, N. C.
Extracts from the Diary of a member of the 19th Regiment.
(Chapter Five)

Sunday, Feb. 12th, 1865 — Windy and cool. Corn-bread and bean-soup. No wood.

Monday, Feb. 13th — Clear and cool. Bread and bean-soup. Three Union officers—prisoners at Danville—arrived here to-day, for the purpose of distributing clothing among the prisoners.—They bring the glad tidings that we will soon be within our own lines, God grant that this may be true.

Tuesday, Feb. 14th — Hazy and cool. Bread and bean-soup. Three cheers for Uncle Sam! Woolen blankets were distributed to us to-day; other articles of clothing will be distributed to-morrow. This is a God send to us, as our sufferings have been terrible.

Wednesday, Feb. 15th — Best morning I have seen since I entered the Confederacy, because of the comfortable sleep I enjoyed last night. If our blankets had arrived two months sooner, the lives of several hundred unfortunate beings would have been saved. Cloudy and cold. Corn-bread and bean-soup.

Thursday, Feb. 16th — Clear and cool. Corn-bread and bean-soup, and a piece of stinking salt-beef.

Friday, Feb. 17th — Foggy and unpleasant. Corn-bread and bean-soup. Rebel General, Bradley S. Johnson, was in Camp nearly the whole day yesterday—a tall, good-looking officer, gentlemanly in his demeanor, and converses freely with the prisoners.

Saturday, Feb. 18th — A beautiful day. A quarter of a loaf of corn-bread and rice-soup. About 500 Union prisoners came in last night, from Georgia and South Carolina—look hard. At night Gen. Johnson and Maj. Gee told us that some of the prisoners here would leave for exchange within forty-eight hours. Clothing distributed by Union officers—10 pairs pants and blouse-coats, and 8 shirts to my squad (of 100 men.)

Sunday, Feb. 19th — A magnificent day. The prisoners who came last night forwarded for exchange this morning. Corn-bread and meat. Some more clothing distributed. Had preaching from a rebel minister—prisoners paid little attention to him.

Monday, Feb. 20th — Pleasant. The sick out of the several hospitals, and the 7th division, left camp to be exchanged.

Tuesday, Feb. 21st — Pleasant. The sick outside the hospital left camp this forenoon.

Wednesday, Feb.22nd.~ Cloudy. During last night we drew rations—two loaves of corn-bread and a half a pound of raw pork to a man. At noon left camp and marched about seven miles on the Greensboro road and camped two miles north of the Yadkin river. Rain during the night. (Under guard. No shelter.)

Thursday, Feb. 23rd — Rain. Marched twelve miles over a very muddy road and camped.

Friday, Feb. 24th — Rain. March sixteen miles and camped one mile north of High Point Female Seminary, at Thomasville.

Saturday, Feb. 25th — Rain. Marched fifteen miles and arrived at Greensboro, N. C., at 1 o'clock P.M. No transportation for us—bivouacked in the woods—lived on hope—for our rations had given out—got wet during the night.

Sunday, Feb. 26th — Rainy A.M., pleasant P.M. Drew a pint of meal, a pint of flour and molasses. Embarked on the cars for Wilmington at noon.

Monday, Feb. 27th — Passed Raleigh at daylight, and arrived at Goldsboro at 12 noon. In the afternoon we were paroled, and took the cars at night. Cloudy.

Tuesday, Feb. 28th — The happiest day of my life. Arrived at the place of exchange at noon. Were received by our Commissioner and marched across Cape Fear river, to the camp of our troops. Here hard-tack, fresh-beef and coffee were issued to us. Started for Wilmington, marched nine miles, over a miserable road through the swamp, and reached town soon after dark. Were quartered in a warehouse, that, apparently, had not been opened since the capture of the place—a large quantity of tobacco, rebel clothing, canned meat, salt, rice and many other articles were found in the several rooms. And didn't the boys go in on their nerve. It was a caution to see them help themselves. I got my share of the spoils; had turtle soup and Scotch Haggis for my supper.

Wednesday, March 1st — Misty. Marched to the depot to draw three days rations—coffee, sugar, soap, hardtack and salt-pork, as much as we wanted. This looks natural again.

Thursday, March 2nd — Misty. About 500 paroled officers and some of the men went north to-day. Many prisoners here, mostly in a horrible condition.

Friday, March 3rd — Foggy. Still in Wilmington. How different this from prison, where famine and starvation reigned—here the necessities of life are bounteously dealt out. To the Almighty, my thanks are due for the preservation of my life during that struggle with misery, hunger and death.

Saturday, March 4th — Abraham Lincoln is this day inaugurated for another Presidential term. We have no doubt he will be able to crush the rebellion, but that he will punish the originators and leaders of it as the law prescribes, we are rather doubting; but if he keeps in mind the many lives lost by rebel bullets and in rebel military pens, he can but hang every conspirator, even if every tree in the South is to be converted into a gallows. Let him look at Salisbury, where 5,021 Union prisoners died of starvation and nakedness in less than five months.

Sunday, March 5th — Cloudy. Still in Wilmington.

Monday, March 6th — Clear. Embarked on the Lady Lang—changed at the bar to the Charles C. Leary, the most miserable transport I have ever seen, and arrived, after a tedious voyage, at Annapolis, Md.

Friday, March 10th — Cold. Disembarked. Received new clothes throughout and new eating utensils. Everybody feels good and so do I. We are new men indeed. The filth of over four months accumulation is washed off, the old clothes, with their "grey backs," are cast away; bean-soup, meat, wheat-bread and coffee fill our empty stomachs. Is not this enough to make one shout for the Stars and Stripes and swear eternal enmity toward Traitors.— Thank God we are now in a land where men are treated as such.

Saturday, March 11th — Started for Benton Barracks, at St. Louis.

(Note—The writer of this diary of prison life says that he thinks it to be the only one kept by any prisoner at Salisbury while he was there. Had he supposed that it would have been given to the public, it would have been made much more specific in many particulars than it is—that, in fact, many of the most awful scenes witnessed there are not noticed at all—having been so indelibly stamped on the memory as to need no daily record to recall them. It has been to me a matter of surprise, as I have copied it, to see how perfectly it was kept amidst such surroundings—every sentence being ready for the press, even to the marks of punctuation. It shows how mind can triumph over suffering from cold and hunger and nakedness, and scenes of destitution and misery all around.

A. D. Richardson, in "Field Dungeon and Escape" says: "When a Subordinate at Salisbury asked the post Commandant, Maj. John H. Gee: 'Shall I give the prisoners full rations?' he replied: 'No G—d d—n them, give them quarter rations!' Yet at this very time, one of our Salisbury friends, a trustworthy and Christian gentleman, assured us in a stolen interview:

'It is within my personal knowledge that the great commissary warehouse, in this town, is filled to the roofs with corn and pork. I know that the prison commissary finds it difficult to obtain storage for his supplies.'

After our escape we learned from personal observation, that the region abounded in corn and pork. Salisbury was a general depot for army supplies.

To call the foul pens where the patients were confined, 'hospitals,' is a perversion of the English tongue. We could not obtain brooms to keep them clean; we could not get cold water to wash the faces of those sick and dying men. In that region, where every farmer's barn yard contained grain stacks, we could not obtain clean straw enough to place under them. More than half the time they were compelled to lie huddled upon the cold, naked filthy floors, without that degree of warmth and cleanliness usually afforded to brutes. The wasted forms and sad, pleading eyes of these sufferers, waiting wearily for the tide of life to waste away—without the commonest comforts, without one word of sympathy or one tear of affection—will never cease to haunt me."

"At all hours of the day and night, on every side, we heard the terrible hack! hack! hack! in whose pneumonic tones, every prisoner seemed to be coughing his life away."

"The last scene of all was the dead cart, with its rigid fonns piled upon each other like logs—the arms swaying, the white, ghastly faces staring, with drooped jaws and stony eyes—while it rattled along, bearing its precious freight just outside the walls, to be thrown in a mass into trenches and covered with a little earth.")

[Articles 16-17 omitted.]

Reedsburg Free Press — November 1, 1872
RECORD OF REEDSBURG IN THE WAR (18)
By S. A. Dwinnell Hospital life.
Extracts from the diary of a member of the 19th Regiment—with notes.

June 26th, 1864 — At Point of Rocks, on the Appomattox, Va. Sick—sent to the Corps Hospital, located a mile and a half from our quarters. The management here is miserable. Soon after dinner the surgeon came into our tent to examine the patients. The worst cases he sent to the General Hospital, and prescribed for others. He hardly took time to inquire into the cases of each, and made prescriptions without knowing much about the diseases.—Surely, were it not for the Christian Commission many would die here for want of medical attendance.

Tuesday, June 28th — Very warm. Terribly dusty. There was preaching in our tent by a member of the Christian Commission.

Wednesday, June 29th — Pleasant. Had a burning fever all day. Sent to the newly established 18th Corps Hospital, four or five miles down towards City Point, on the South of the Appomattox.

Thursday, June 30th — Pleasant. Was pretty sick all day. Feel very weak.

Friday, July 1st — Capt. Nichols, Sergt. T. Elliott and Corp. Gates brought in wounded, last night.

Saturday, July 2nd — Very warm. The dust is unendurable. Feel considerably better.

Sunday, July 3rd — Pleasant. Very weak.

Monday, July 4th — Warm. Quite weak. No appetite.

(Note.—The Corps Hospitals usually consist of from fifteen to twenty large tents, capable of holding from eight to ten cots each, arranged on each side of a central aisle. Two tents pitched side by side and opening into each other, constituted a ward, under the charge of a ward master. Chronic and obstinate cases of the sick, and the severely wounded, were forwarded from these to the General Hospitals.)

Thursday, July 7th — Warm. Transferred to the 10th Corps Hospital, at Point of Rocks. This hospital appears much better than the 18th Corps.

(Note.—The 19th Regiment was temporarily connected with the 10th Corps at this time, and for this reason the transfer was allowed. Dr. Porter, from a Connecticut Regiment, was appointed assistant surgeon here. He was a thorough, active fellow, and put wrongs to rights at a fast rate. He found some of the nurses and convalescent officers who messed together, using portions of the sanitary stores intended for the sick. He put a stop to these abuses at once — told the officers that the Government paid them for supplying their own table, and if they were known taking sanitary stores again he would report them to be cashiered.

The Christian Commission had, among its agents there, a Miss Perkins, a sprightly girl who, accompanied by a colored boy with a basket of various kinds of fruit, apples, peaches, lemons and oranges, passed through the Hospital quite frequently, distributing her gifts, under the direction of the ward master, to the patients, according to their needs. On Sunday her basket was filled with religious reading, writing paper, envelopes and stationary, for gratuitous distribution to patients.)

Saturday, July 9th — Cloudy and cool. Feel weak. The Doctor prescribed low diet; that is, toast for breakfast, toast for dinner and toast for supper. I am well satisfied with it.

Sunday, July 10th — Very warm. No better. Have eggs with our toast.

Monday, July 11th — Very warm. Slowly improving.

Tuesday, July 12th — The doctor is doping me with quinine, which makes me feel quite sick.

Saturday, July 16th — The sick are continually coming in. Am better—Should I continue to improve, as for two days past, shall start for the front Monday morning.

Sunday, July 17th — Morning cool. Divine service at 3 P.M. Do not feel as well.

Monday, July 18th — Burning fever. The doctor chalked me down for an extra dose of quinine; the only medicine I have taken since I came here. Seems to do me more harm than good.

Tuesday, July 19th — Rains most of the day. The Doctor has changed my medicine at last. No quinine—continued head-ache—appetite good. Nice fare here—soft bread, good coffee and tea, butter often. For dinner we have soup or meat, potatoes and pickles. The lady nurses are all gone, much to the chagrin of the sick.

(Note.—The lady nurses were in the employ of the Sanitary Commission and were sometimes removed from one Hospital to another. Among them was a widow whose husband had been an officer in the Army of the West. She accompanied him, and in caring for the wounded, had twice been wounded herself—once severely in the foot or ankle, which caused her to limp in walking. She was a noble woman and an excellent nurse. The sick became much attached to her.)

Wednesday, July 20th — The new doctor seems to be doing well—think he will soon straighten me out.

Thursday, July 21st — Heartily sick of hospital life. Wish I could go to the front. Some of the boys are wounded and brought in nearly every time they are on duty in the trenches.

Sunday, July 24th — Our new physician is doing well. Boys all improving. Some going to their regiments every day.

Monday, July 25th — Left 18th Corps Hospital, walked across the Appomattox (River), some three or four miles, to the 10th Corps Hospital. Rode in ambulance five or six miles to field hospital of the 19th Regiment, and from there walked two miles to the camp of the 19th. Feel very weak.

Tuesday, July 26th — Unwell.

Wednesday, July 27th — Feel worse.

Sunday, July 31st — Went to our field hospital—stopped about fifteen minutes—and proceeded by ambulance, about seven miles to the 18th Corps Hospital. The ride made me quite sick.

(Note.—The field hospital consisted of several large hospital tents, suitable for eight or ten cots each, and a large number of fly tents, open at each end. Cots are provided for the severely sick and wounded only. The others lay upon straw. The small tents will hold from ten to fifteen, and the large ones from twenty to thirty each. The severely sick and wounded are forwarded to the field hospitals—ambulances running continually for that purpose.)

(Note.—Dr. Devendorf, surgeon of the 19th Regiment, from Delavan, was appointed Medical Director of the 18th Corps at this time, and came down to the hospital in his blouse and slouch hat, without any insignia of his office upon his person, on a tour of inspection. He found several young surgeons having a soldier, with a flesh wound in his arm, upon the dissecting table, preparing to amputate. Dr. D. looked on and quietly remarked, "that arm can be saved." The surgeons paid little attention to the remark and were again preparing their knives, when he spoke again, more sternly, "that arm can be saved." They then stopped and made another examination, probing the wound. There was no bone broken, but they again decided to take off the arm. Dr. D. then spoke with authority, "that arm shall be saved." The young surgeons then looked up and enquired, "and who are you?" Dr. D. replied, "I am Medical Inspector of the 18th Army Corps." The young surgeons dropped their knives and concluded to dress the wound and save the limb.)

Monday, Aug. 8th — Very warm. After dinner embarked on hospital steamer, Monitor, and proceeded down the James river. This boat is fitted up with cots and all the appendages of a general hospital.

Tuesday, Aug. 9th — Warm.—Landed, went ashore and took quarters in Ward number two, Hampton General Hospital. Am quite comfortable. Have good clean bed, beef-steak, potatoes, bread and tea for dinner; bread, butter, apple sauce and tea or gruel for supper.

Friday, Aug 12th — Feel right smart. Had toasted-bread, codfish, ham and coffee for breakfast; rice and milk, potatoes, fried-onions, beef and bread for dinner; bread butter, applesauce and tea for supper.

Saturday, Aug. 13th — Not as well. Heat unendurable. Two men died in our Ward to-day. In the afternoon a party of six gentlemen and five ladies went through the several wards and sang two pieces of sacred music. One of the men read several passages of Scripture.

Monday, Aug. 15th — Started for Wisconsin with the 19th Regiment, which goes on Veteran furlough.

(Note.—Hampton Hospital consisted of twenty-five long wooden buildings each one story in height. Each building was a ward. In one part was a cook room, a dispensary and officers' and nurses' rooms. The remainder was filled with cots arranged on each side of a central aisle. Many hospital tents were in use on the grounds for the convalescents—the whole accommodating many hundred patients.

In the Corps Hospitals there were convalescent camps, where soldiers pitched their own tents, and many of them were employed in police and other duties.)

Reedsburg Free Press - June 28, 1872
THE DEAD OF REEDSBURG IN THE WAR OF THE REBELLION! (1)

There appears to be no list of those from this town, who fell in the late war, yet made out. Believing it to be due to the memory of those who sacrificed their lives in defence of their country, as well as to the future historian of the town that such a record be made, I have taken considerable pains to perfect one. This required a good deal of labor, some of the names not appearing in the Adjutant General's report of our dead, others being misspelled. It is possible that I have failed to report all; if so, let any person having a knowledge of the facts, send to me, and I will add to this list. Wm. Miller enlisted from Winfield, WI but removed his family to this town. Hugh Collins and J. Wesley Dickens died after their discharge, from disease contracted in the army. Three families lost two each: Collins, father and son; and Miles and Pitts, two sons each.

After the following names, k stands for killed in action, w for died of wounds, and d for died of disease. The number before the name indicates the regiment.

INFANTRY

6.   Geo. C. Miles, k, South Mountain, Md., Sept. 14, 1862
7.   Geo. W. Root, d, Arlington, Va., Feb. 28, 1862
11. Amariah Robotham, d, Pocahontas, Ark., May 8, 1862
12. Serg't Spencer S. Miles, w, Marietta, Ga. July 26, 1864
12. Serg't F. W. Henry, k, Atlanta, Ga., July 22, 1864
12. J. Wesley Dickens, d, LaValle, Wis.
12. Charles T. Pollock, d, Bolivar, Tenn., Nov. 30, 1862

12. Chas. Reifenrath, k, Kenesaw (Kennesaw) Mt., Ga., June 27, 1864

19. Serg't A. P. Steese, d, Hampton, Va., July 20, 1864

19. Corp. Alvah Rathbun, w, Fortress Monroe, Va., Nov. 5, 1864

19. Dexter C. Cole, d, Madison, Wis., March, 1864 (March 7, 1863, ten days after enlistment)

19. Hugh Collins, d, Reedsburg, Wis., Aug., 1867

19. John Cary, d, Portsmouth, Va., Feb. 19, 1863

19. Charles Day, w, Hampton, Va., June 16, 1864

19. Dexter Green, k, Fair Oaks, Va., Oct. 27, 1864

19. Ephraim Haines, w, Portsmouth, Va., July 5, 1864

19. Wm. D. Hobby, d, Yorktown, Va., July 31, 1863

19. Wm. Horsch, d, Hampton, Va., July 29, 1864

19. James Markee, d, Portsmouth, Va., Oct. 12, 1862

19. Wm. Miller, w, Richmond, Va., Nov. 1, 1864

19. Newman W. Pitts, d, Salisbury Prison, N.C., Jan. 16, 1865

19. Benj. S. Pitts, k, Drury's (Drewry's) Bluff, Va., May 16, 1864

23. Erastus Miller, k, Blakely, Ala., April 8, 1865

23. Jason W. Shaw, k, Vicksburg, Miss., May 28, 1863

23. John Waltz, d, Memphis, Tenn., March 9, 1863

49. John McIlvaine, d, Reedsburg, Wis., March 3, 1865

CAVALRY

1. Erastus H. Knowles, d, St. Louis, Mo., April 8, 1862

3. Henry Bulow, k, Baxter Springs, Ark., (KS), Oct. 6, 1863

3. Geo. W. Priest, d, Camp Bowen, Ark., Nov. 6, 1862

1st Mo. Battery. John Collins, d, Cincinnati, Oh., Aug., 1862

—N.Y. Regt. Boardman Roscoe, Davids Is., N.Y., Apr. 1865

Unknown. Holden Miller, Madison, Wis., 1864

From this list we find that Reedsburg lost a larger number than any one supposed, being about one-fourth of all who enlisted. Of these, eight were killed, six died of wounds, and eighteen of disease. The 19th Regiment took more from this town than any other, and consequently lost more.

Henry Bulow was murdered, with all the Regimental Band of the 3rd Cavalry, after surrender, and their bodies thrown under the Band Wagon and burned, by order of the infamous (William C.) Quantrill, who, with 500 rebels, were disguised in Federal uniforms.

S. A. Dwinnell.

Reedsburg, Wisconsin, June 24th, 1872

New York Tribune, Wednesday, April 19, 1865
(price of the paper 5 cents)
From North Carolina
General Stoneman's Brilliant Raid
He occupies Salisbury, North Carolina
19 guns 1,165 Prisoners taken
(War Department,
Washington Tuesday, April 18, 1865)

    Colonel Palmer attacked, and after some fighting, captured Wythesville, destroyed the depot of supplies at that point, and also at Malis Meadow. Major Wagner, after striking the railroad at Big Lick, pushed on toward Lynchburg, destroying on his way the important bridges over the Big and Little Otter, and got to within four miles of Lynchburg. With the main body I effectually destroyed the road between New River and Big Lick, and then struck for Greensborough, on the North Carolina railroad. Arrived near Salem, North Carolina, I detailed Palmer's brigade to destroy the bridges between Danville and Greensborough, and between Greensborough and Yadkin River, and the large depots of supplies along the road.
    This duty was performed with considerable fighting, the capture of 400 prisoners, and to my entire satisfaction. With the other two brigades, Brown and Miller's, and the artillery under the command of Lt. Reagon, we pushed for Salisbury where we found about 3,000 troops under the command of Major General W. M. Gardiner, and 14 pieces of artillery under command of Colonel (later Lt-General) Pemberton.

The whole formed behind Grant's Creek, about two miles and a half from Salisbury. As soon as a proper disposition could be made, I ordered a general charge along the entire line, and the result was the capture of the whole 14 pieces of artillery, 1,364 prisoners, including 54 officers.

All the artillery and 1,164 prisoners are now with us. The remainder of the force was chased through and several miles beyond the town, but scattered and escaped into the woods.

We remained in Salisbury two days, during which time we destroyed 15 miles of railroad track and the bridges toward Charlotte, and then moved to this point.

Note: General Stoneman led 6,000 cavalrymen into North Carolina and Virginia to disrupt the enemy, destroy ironworks, public buildings, etc. as he went. He planned to free prisoners at Salisbury but when he entered Salisbury he destroyed the deserted prison camp there. The people of Salisbury still talk about the destruction of the buildings that occurred at that time.

At this time Generals Sherman and Johnson had signed an agreement which called for an armistice by all armies in the field.

President Lincoln had died on April 15th and Andrew Johnson assumed the office of Presidency.

CHAPTER 5

- Photograph of Nelson Gardner—circa 1905

- Unsung Hero

- Copy of Aberdeen News, dated September 7, 1907
  (pictures of Nanseumon River, Virginia)

- A Review of the Heroic Act—Company A, 19th Regiment

- Letter N. J. House

Photograph of Nelson Gardner circa 1905

UNSUNG HERO

The copy of the Aberdeen Daily newspaper dated September 7, 1907 tells of the heroic act of Nelson Gardner. The many articles of Civil War history verifies the details of the act.

The family states that the Medal of Honor was received just after his death in 1909. The uniform of Nelson Gardner had been donated to the local library with the understanding they would be displayed in the new museum in Aberdeen, SD. The uniform and Medal have not been located.

The obituary also states that Nelson had received an injury which resulted in his head being carried at a slight angle the rest of his life.

The Medal has not been noted in the U. S. Military records. I have written to National Archives and Records Administration in DC and there is no government record of his receiving this Medal of Honor.

One military contact suggested I write to a congressman. I sent the information to the Congresswoman in SD. I felt it would certainly be of interest to her State. The material was forwarded on to my local Congressman and confirmation has not been made.

Many instances verify that this young man was brave, diligent, and eager to serve his country at all risks   I'm sure there were many men fighting this Great War who are Unsung Heroes. We're proud of Nelson Slater Gardner and the others that served our country during this time....

Effie Leatherman, Author

SECOND SECTION — ABERDEEN DAILY NEWS — PAGES 7 TO 12
ESTABLISHED JULY, 1886 — ABERDEEN, SOUTH DAKOTA, SATURDAY, SEPTEMBER 7, 1907 — EVENING EDITION

Nelson Gardner's Heroic Act Will Win Him A Congressional Medal

DARING DEED IN CIVIL WAR BY AN ABERDEEN MAN WILL BE REWARDED

If a brave act, performed in the face of the greatest danger—when the chances of death are overwhelming—entitles the hero to a medal for bravery, then Nelson Gardner of this city, a veteran of the civil war, should have one, and he will if the Grand Army of the Republic can secure it for him.

Comrades Tell the Story

Nelson Gardner, who was a private in Company A of the Nineteenth Wisconsin Infantry volunteers, and Hephron Hanes, a comrade in the same company, performed one of the bravest acts on record in the civil war. Nelson Gardner does not say so; he is too modest, but his comrades—that is, all who are left—relate the story. It was told at a reunion of the old regiment during the recent G. A. R. encampment in Minneapolis and again at the meeting of all the veterans at which the commandant of the regiment submitted a resolution reciting the heroic act of Nelson Gardner and asking the G. A. R. to take the necessary steps to bring the matter before congress so that, even at this late day, the medal for bravery might be given to Comrade Gardner.

Gardner's Comrade Killed

Hephron Hanes was killed a few [illegible] after he and his comrade had [illegible] been made.

Nelson Gardner enlisted at the age of 15 years at Reedsburg, Wis. Less than two years later his regiment was in a brigade marching along the [illegible] on fuller. On the opposite bank, concealed by tall grass and weeds, the rebels lay concealed and firing with deadly effect into the ranks of their enemy.

Must Dislodge Enemy

Everything was done to dislodge the confederates but without success and scores of union soldiers fell in that valley of death. A halt was ordered. Too many men had already been killed and many more would be shot down before it could be possible to get out of range of the sharpshooters on the other bank. It became necessary to dislodge the enemy, but how? If it were possible to set fire to the dry brush across the river the danger would be over. Other plans were thought out but none appeared feasible except the one mentioned.

Two Heroes Volunteered

Finally the colonel placed the matter before the officers and the officers told the men. The colonel wanted some man to swim the river and set fire to the brush. He would not detail anybody to perform the task for it seemed like certain death, but he called for volunteers. There were several responses but at the eleventh hour only two men remained firm in their determination to tempt death [illegible] ing, but their colonel's wish[illegible]

Death in Order

Receiving their instructions, these two men discarded their clothing, and placing a supply of matches in their hair waded into the river. Hiding

COMRADE'S AFFIDAVIT TO THE STORY

State of South Dakota, County of Lincoln, ss.

N. J. House being duly sworn says: That he resides in Canton, Lincoln county, South Dakota, and that is his postoffice address. That he was a private in Co. D, 19th Wis. Infty. Vols.; that he was present with the regiment during the month of April, 1863, when it was stationed on the Nansumon river and the rifle pits located there; that there was a rebel battery on the opposite side of the river and about three-quarters of a mile away, that between the rebel battery and the river there was a marsh of tall grass and weeds; that the rebels would come out through the grass and weeds and being concealed by the grass [illegible] weeds they would shoot our men. Several attempts were made [illegible] colonel to set the grass on fire [illegible] failed.

Nelson Gardner of [illegible] and Hephron Hanes, volunteered to swim the river and set the grass on fire. The colonel said it was so dangerous that he would not order the men to go, but if they volunteered he would like to have them go. They stripped off their clothes, put some matches in their hair, swam the river and set the grass on fire; on their return they were fired upon many times and as Hanes was ascending the bank he was wounded and died soon after from his wounds. We were not after that annoyed by the rebel sharpshooters.

This was the most dangerous, daring and heroic act that I saw during the war. I was present and saw the above described brave act.

I have no interest in this matter and make this affidavit from my personal observation and voluntarily.

—N. J. House.

Subscribed and sworn to before me this 15th day of December, 1906, and I certify that I am personally acquainted with N. J. House who subscribed the foregoing affidavit and that he understood its contents before execution and that he is a credible witness and that I have no interest in this case.

—J. V. Conklin,
Notary Public, Lincoln Co., S. D.

[illegible] the other side and crawling up the bank and into the brush. [illegible] match after match until the dry weeds caught fire and the flames began to spread. When they were sure their task had been accomplished the two [illegible] to swim [illegible] bullets [illegible] and [illegible] about them and they dived several times for safety. They reached the bank, eager to rush out of the terrible rain of bullets but only one man reached the union lines alive. Hephron Hanes was shot in the side just as he was clambering up the bank. The bullet went through his body and he fell mortally wounded. Gardner picked him up and assisted by union soldiers who ran to his assistance, the wounded man was carried into safety, only to die a few minutes later.

BRAVES DEATH BY SWIMMING RIVER AND DISLODGING EMEMY FROM BRUSH

Fire Dislodges Enemy

In the meantime the fire across the river had spread and soon a large area of brush was destroyed and with it the hiding place of the confederates. The work was well done. The danger was over and the brigade proceeded on its march. This was the act performed by Hephron Hanes and Nelson Gardner for which the Grand Army of the Republic believes congress will award a medal.

17 Years Old But a Man

Nelson Gardner at that time was less than 17 years of age, but boys were men in those days. In October, 1864, he was taken prisoner and confined in Libby prison, where he underwent all the hardships which made that place notorious.

After six months in Libby he was sent to the stockades at Salisbury, N. C., where additional sufferings were heaped upon the prisoners. Herded together like cattle, they received half a pint of meal a day for subsistence. Gardner traded all he had for food. The buttons of his uniform went one by one, then some trinkets he had carefully guarded and finally his tunic. He will not talk of the sufferings of those days. They are still fresh in his memory although they happened forty odd years ago.

Medal Is Promised

The story of Nelson Gardner's heroism has been told to the congressional delegation from Wisconsin and the promise is given that the coveted medal for distinguished bravery will be awarded to this veteran.

Nelson Gardner is well known in this city. He has hosts of friends and all will be glad when the news comes that his heroism has been rewarded by an appreciative government.

A TRAMP IN COMMAND

(Copyright, 1907, by [illegible])

During the Cuban revolution the American ship Curlew, carrying arms and ammunition to the Cubans, had among the crew a dissipated man entered by the name of Jones. He had been a tramp along the water front. He had conversed with sailors. He knew all about first mates and second mates. To have "back talked" would have been to admit a broken [illegible] [illegible]

[illegible]

HEARD HERE AND THERE

A stranger, afflicted with the habit of stuttering, accosted a man on Main street, near Second avenue, yesterday [illegible]

[illegible]

The alleys have been attacked and many backyards have been made [illegible]

Aberdeen Daily News-September 7, 1907

Nelson Gardner's Heroic Act
Will Win Him a Congressional Medal

If a brave act, performed in the face of the greatest danger-when the chances of death are overwhelming entitles the hero to a medal for bravery, then Nelson Gardner of this city, a veteran of this city, a veteran of the Civil War, should have one, and he will if the Grand Army of the Republic can secure it for him.

Comrades Tell The Story

Nelson Gardner, who was a private in Company A of the Nineteenth Wisconsin Infantry volunteers, and Hephron Hanes, a comrade in the same company, performed one of the greatest acts on record in the Civil War. Nelson Gardner does not say so, he is too modest, but his comrades-that is, who are all left, relate the story. It was told at a reunion of the old regiment during the recent G. A. R. encampment in Minneapolis and again at the meeting of the veterans at which the remnant of the regiment submitted a resolution reciting the heroic act of Nelson Gardner and asking the G. A. R. to take the necessary steps to bring the matter before congress so that, even at this late day, the medal for bravery might be given to Comrade Gardner.

Gardner's Comrade Killed

Hephron Hanes was killed a few minutes after he and his comrade had ------- (Illegible)

Nelson Gardner enlisted at the age of 15 years at Reedsburg, Wis. Less than two years later his regiment was in a brigade operating along the Nansumon river and it was there one of the hardest parts of the campaign was faced by this brigade of the Union force. On the opposite bank, concealed by tall grass and weeds, the rebels lay concealed and firing with great effects into the ranks of their enemy.

Must Dislodge the Enemy

Everything was done to dislodge the confederates but without success and scores of union soldiers fell in that valley of death. A halt was ordered. Too many men had already been killed and many more would be shot down before it would be possible to get out of range of the sharpshooters on the other bank. It became necessary to dislodge the enemy but how? If it were possible to set fire to the dry brush across the river the danger would be over. Other plans were thought out but none appeared feasible except the mentioned.

Two Heroes Volunteered

Finally the colonel placed the matter before the officers and the officers told the men. The colonel wanted some men to swim the river and set fire to the brush. He would not detail anybody to perform the task for it seemed like certain death, but he called for volunteers. There were several responses but at the eleventh hour only two men remained firm in their determination to tempt death by carrying out their colonel's wishes and that was Hephron Hanes and Nelson Gardner.

Death is Defied

Receiving their instructions these two men discarded their clothing, and placing a supply of matches in their hair, waded into the river. How they swam across without being struck by a bullet is one of the miracles of the civil war. They reached the other side and crawling up the bank and into the brush. Lit match after match until the dry weeds caught fire and the flames began to spread. When they were sure their task had been accomplished they began to swim back to the other side.

Bullets were (illegible) and about them and they dived several times for safety. They reached the bank eager to rush out of the terrible rain of bullets but only one man reached the union lines alive. Heprhon Hanes was shot in the side just as he was clambering up the bank. The bullet went through his body and he fell mortally wounded. Gardner picked him up and assisted by union soldiers who ran to his assistance, the wounded man was carried into safety, only to die a few minutes later

Fire Dislodges Enemy

In the meantime the fire across the river had spread and soon a large area of brush was destroyed and with it the hiding place of the confederates. The work was well done. The danger was over and the brigade proceeded on its march. This was the act performed by Hephron Hanes and Nelson Gardner for which the Grand Army of the Republic believes congress will award a medal.

17 Years Old But a Man

Nelson Gardner at that time was less than 17 years of age, but boys were men in those day. In October, 1864, he was taken prisoner and confined to Libbey prison where he underwent all the hardships which made that place notorious.

After six months in Libbey he was sent to the stockades at Salisbury, N.C. where additional sufferings were heaped upon the prisoners. Herded together like cattle, they received half a pint of meal a day for substances. Gardner traded all he had for food. The buttons of the uniform went one by one, then some trinkets he had carefully guarded and finally his tunic. He will not talk of the sufferings of those days. They are still fresh in his memory although they happened forty odd years ago.

Medal is Promised

The story of Nelson Gardner's heroism has been told to the congressional delegation from Wisconsin and the promise is given that the coveted medal for distinguished bravery will be awarded to this veteran.

Nelson Gardner is well known in this city. He has hosts of friends and all will be glad when the news comes that his heroism has been rewarded by an appreciative government.

BRAVES DEATH BY SWIMMING RIVER AND DISLODGING EMEMY FROM BRUSH

ron Hanes was shot in the side just as he was clambering up the bank. The bullet went through his body and he fell mortally wounded. Gardner picked him up and assisted by union soldiers who ran to his assistance, the wounded man was carried into safety, only to die a few minutes later.

Fire Dislodges Enemy

In the meantime the fire across the river had spread and soon a large area of brush was destroyed and with it the hiding place of the confederates. The work was well done. The danger was over, and the brigade proceeded on its march. This was the act performed by Hephron Hanes and Nelson Gardner for which the Grand Army of the Republic believes congress will award a medal.

17 Years Old But a Man

Nelson Gardner at that time was less than 17 years of age, but boys were men in those days. In October, 1864, he was taken prisoner and confined in Libbey prison where he underwent all the hardships which made that place notorious.

After six months in Libbey he was sent to the stockades at Salisbury, N. C., where additional sufferings were heaped upon the prisoners. Herded together like cattle, they received half a pint of meal a day for subsistence. Gardner traded all he had for food. The buttons of his uniform went one by one, then some trinkets he had carefully guarded and finally his tunic. He will not talk of the sufferings of those days. They are still fresh in his memory although they happened forty odd years ago.

Medal is Promised

The story of Nelson Gardner's heroism has been told to the congressional delegation from Wisconsin and the promise is given that the coveted medal for distinguished bravery will be awarded to this veteran.

Nelson Gardner is well known in this city. He has hosts of friends and all will be glad when the news comes that his heroism has been rewarded by an appreciative government.

DARING DEED IN CIVIL WAR BY AN ABERDEEN MAN WILL BE REWARDED

If a brave act, performed in the face of the greatest danger—when the chances of death are overwhelming—entitles the hero to a medal for bravery, then Nelson Gardner of this city, a veteran of the civil war, should have one, and he will if the Grand Army of the Republic can secure it for him.

Comrades Tell the Story

Nelson Gardner, who was a private in Company A of the Nineteenth Wisconsin Infantry volunteers, and Hephron Hanes, a comrade in the same company, performed one of the bravest acts on record in the civil war. Nelson Gardner does not say so; he is too modest, but his comrades—that is, all who are left—relate the story. It was told at a reunion of the old regiment during the recent G. A. R. encampment in Minneapolis and again at the meeting of all the veterans at which the remnant of the regiment submitted a resolution reciting the heroic act of Nelson Gardner and asking the G. A. R. to take the necessary steps to bring the matter before congress so that, even at this late day, the medal for bravery might be given to Comrade Gardner.

Gardner's Comrade Killed

Hephron Hanes was killed a few ... after he and his comrade had ...

other hero's medal.

Nelson Gardner enlisted at the age of 15 years at Reedsburg, Wis. Less than two years later his regiment was in a brigade operating along the Nansumon river and it was there one ion force. On the opposite bank, concealed by tall grass and woods, the rebels lay concealed and firing with cruel effect into the ranks of their enemy.

Must Dislodge Enemy

Everything was done to dislodge the confederates but without success and scores of union soldiers fell in that valley of death. A halt was ordered. Too many men had already been killed and many more more would be shot down before it could be possible to get out of range of the sharpshooters on the other bank. It became necessary to dislodge the enemy, but how? If it were possible to set fire to the dry brush across the river the danger would be over. Other plans were thought out but none appeared feasible except the one mentioned.

Two Heroes Volunteered

Finally the colonel placed the matter before the officers and the officers told the men. The colonel wanted some men to swim the river and set fire to the brush. He would not detail anybody to perform the task for it seemed like certain death, but he called for volunteers. There were several responses but at the eleventh hour only two men remained firm in their determination to tempt death by carrying out their colonel's wishes. These were Nelson Gardner...

Death In Defiance

Receiving their instructions, these two men discarded their clothing, and placing a supply of matches in their hair, waded into the river. How they swam across without being

Letter N. J. House

N. J. House being duly sworn says, that he resides in Canton, Lincoln County South Dakota and that is his post office address. That he was a private in Co. D 12 Wis. Inf'y Vols. That he was present with the regiment during the time of April 1863 while it was stationed on the Nansemon river and the pits located there; that there was a Rebel battery on the opposite side the river and about three quarters of a mile away, that between this rebel battery and the river there was a marsh of tall grass and weeds; that the rebels would come out through the grass and well hid being concealed in the grass and would they attempt were made by our Colonel to set the grass on fire, but failed.

Nelson Gardner of Co. "A" and .... offered ....in the ..... to set the grass on fire. He would not order this men to, but if they volunteered, would like to have them go. They stripped off their clothes, placed some matches in their hair, swam the river and set the grass on fire, on their return they were fired upon many times and as he was ascending the bank he was wounded and died soon after from his wounds. We were not after that annoyed by the rebel sharpshooters.

This was the most dangerous, daring and heroic act that I saw during the war. I was present and saw the described brave act.

I have no interest in this matter I make this affidavit from my personal observation.

N. J. House.

Subscribed and sworn to before me ...day of December 1905 and I certify that I am personally acquainted with N. J. House who subscribed the foregoing affidavit and that he read its contents before ex...... that he ...... a credible ...... has no interest in this case.

Notary Public, Lincoln Co., S. D.

River Crossing Where Nelson and Hanes Sent the Confederates a Flee with Fire.

CHAPTER 6

- End of Life — Nelson Slater Gardner (January 1, 1846 — July 24, 1909)

- His Civil War Momentos

- Genealogy

- Margaret Craft and the Family Croft Castle

- My Notes — Effie E. Leatherman, author

End of Life — Nelson Slater Gardner
January 1, 1846 — July 24, 1909)

Effie Leatherman

The Aberdeen Daily News, Monday, July 26, 1909

(Article Enlargements on pages that follow)

THE ABERDEEN DAILY NEWS, MONDAY, JULY 26, 1909

REEDSBURG, WISCONSIN,

DEATH OF NELSON GARDNER.

Lived in Reedsburg. Veteran of Civil War.

Nelson Gardner was buried July 25, at Aberdeen, S. D. His death was caused by paralysis.

Mr. Gardner formerly lived about three miles west of Reedsburg near the Krueger farm. From there he enlisted in Dec. 1861 in Co. A, 19th Wis. Inf. After the war he moved to Iowa, and later to Dakota and is survived by his wife, one son and one daughter. The deceased saw much real war service. He was at one time guard of rebel prisoners and was himself taken prisoner and put in Libby prison. At the battle of Fair Oaks he was severely wounded. He was awarded a medal for bravery in swimming the river at Suffolk carrying matches in his teeth and setting fire to some dry grass in which the enemy lay concealed. He, with his companion were under heavy fire all the time but returned uninjured. It will be remembered that it was this regiment which was before Petersburg and Fair Oaks, at the latter place 190 men went into action and only 44 came back.

NELSON GARDNER IS NOW AT REST

FUNERAL OF CIVIL WAR VETERAN HELD YESTERDAY AFTERNOON

The funeral of the late Nelson S. Gardner was held yesterday afternoon from the M. E. church and was very largely attended, for the deceased possessed a large circle of friends. The sermon by Rev. Dr. J. W. Taylor was adapted to the last rites for a soldier of the Civil war, and he pronounced a very good one. At Riverside the G. A. R. had charge of the services and Captain J. H Hanover gave a short talk on the comrade who had left the post. The women of the W. R. C. and the members of the G. A. R. were in attendance. Among the out of town relatives present were Mrs. Effie Fritz, a daughter, of Kansas City, Mo.; Mrs. Jane Martin, a sister, and Henry Gardner, a brother, of Chetak, Wis.; Mrs. Alice Markham of Miles City, Mont., and Mrs. Maud Record, a neice, of Darrel, Minn.

The pall bearers were M. Brooks, J. W. Smith, H. C. Chase, T. B. Wells, J. W. Jaques and T. Boardman.

Mr. Gardner enlisted in the union army in December, 1861, and was a member of Company A, Nineteenth Wisconsin infantry. Until the following July the regiment acted as guard to rebel prisoners when they were ordered to Norfolk, W. Va. In April, 1863, his regiment was ordered to Suffolk and it was there Mr. Gardner, with a fellow soldier, swam the river under fire and set fire to the high grass which concealed the rebels. This regiment saw service at Petersburg, was in the battle of Fair Oaks where out of 190 men who went to battle only forty-two came back. Mr. Gardner was in Libby prison, and in the prisons at Danville and Salisbury. At the battle of Fair Oaks, in October, 1864, Mr. Gardner received a wound in the head which caused him to carry his head in the fashion with which his friends are familiar, the bullet so affecting him that he was never able to hold his head erect.

THE ABERDEEN DAILY NEWS, SATURDAY, JULY 24, 1909

DEATH TAKES N. S. GARDNER

GALLANT SOLDIER OF THE CIVIL WAR SUCCUMBS TO STROKE OF PARALYSIS

Nelson S. Gardner, who had a stroke of paralysis a week ago, died today at his home at 11:15. He received the stroke just a week ago today at 11:15, being ill just exactly seven days.

Mr. Gardner has been in fairly good health up to a week ago, when he was stricken with paralysis while superintending a gang of men at the Culbertsand pit, and came back to town. He sank into a stupor and his condition improved but little since then, his age retarding recovery.

Mr. Gardner was 63 years old last January and had lived in South Dakota for twenty-seven years, and in Aberdeen for the past eleven years, when he moved in from his farm northeast of this city. He has held many prominent positions in the G. A. R., and was commander here a few years ago. He was in the civil war, serving four years, in the Nineteenth Wisconsin regiment. During the war he made an enviable record by his bravery and had been awarded a medal by congress for his bravery in swimming across the Nansemon river under a heavy fire from the enemy and setting fire to the grass on the other side. The medal was awarded to him several months ago but he had not received it yet at the time of his death.

Mr. Gardner was born in Pennsylvania, but moved from there while very young and went to Wisconsin, where he hs early boyhood was spent. Later on he moved to Iowa, where he was married in 1868 to Margaret E. Kraft, who survives him. He settled in South Dakota in 1881 and has lived here ever since.

He leaves besides his widow, a son, Elmer Gardner of Aberdeen, and a daughter, Mrs. Effie Fritz of Kansas City. He also has a sister, Mrs. Alice Markham of Rapid City, and a brother, Henry Gardner of Chetak, Wis.

Mr. Gardner was well known in this part of the state and was respected by all who knew him. He had held prominent positions in the city, being city weighmaster up to a few weeks ago.

The funeral will take place at 3 o'clock tomorrow afternoon at the Methodist church, and will be in charge of the G. A. R. The members of the G. A. R. and the W. R. C. will meet at the house at 2:30 and escort the remains to the church. Services by Rev. J. W. Taylor. Interment will be in Riverside, and members of the G. A. R. will act as pall bearers.

tives present were Mrs. Effie Fritz, a daughter, of Kansas City, Mo.; Mrs. Jane Martin, a sister, and Henry Gardner, a brother, of Chetak, Wis.; Mrs. Alice Markham of Miles City, Mont., and Mrs. Maud Record, a neice, of Dassel, Minn.

The pall bearers were M. Brooks, J. W. Smith, H. C. Chase, T. B. Wells, J. W. Jaques and T. Boardman.

Mr. Gardner enlisted in the union army in December, 1861, and was a member of Company A, Nineteenth Wisconsin infantry. Until the following July the regiment acted as guard to rebel prisoners when they were ordered to Norfolk, W. Va. In April, 1863, his regiment was ordered to Suffolk and it was there Mr. Gardner, with a fellow soldier, swam the river under fire and set fire to the high grass which concealed the rebels. This regiment saw service at Petersburg, was in the battle of Fair Oaks, where out of 130 men who went to battle only forty-four came back. Mr. Gardner was in Libby prison, and in the prisons at Danville and Salisbury. At the battle of Fair Oaks, in October, 1864, Mr. Gardner received a wound in the head which caused him to carry his head in the fashion with which his friends are familiar, the bullet so affecting him that he was never able to hold his head erect.

DEATH TAKES N. S. GARDNER

GALLANT SOLDIER OF THE CIVIL WAR SUCCUMBS TO STROKE OF PARALYSIS

Nelson S. Gardner, who had a stroke of paralysis a week ago, died today at his home at 11:15. He received the stroke just a week ago today at 11:15, being ill just exactly seven days.

Mr. Gardner has been in fairly good health up to a week ago, when he was stricken with paralysis while superintending a gang of men at the Culbert sand pit, and came back to town. He sank into a stupor and his condition improved but little since then, his age retarding recovery.

Mr. Gardner was 63 years old last January and had lived in South Dakota for twenty-seven years, and in Aberdeen for the past eleven years, when he moved in from his farm northeast of this city. He has held many prominent positions in the G. A. R. and was commander here a few years ago. He was in the civil war, serving four years, in the Nineteenth Wisconsin regiment. During the war he made an enviable record by his bravery and coolness in time of danger and had been awarded a medal by congress for his bravery in swimming across the Nansamon river under a heavy fire from the enemy, and setting fire to the grass on the other side. The medal was awarded to him several months ago but he had not received it yet at the time of his death.

Mr. Gardner was born in Pennsylvania, but moved from there while very young and went to Wisconsin, where he is early boyhood was spent. Later on he moved to Iowa, where he was married in 1866 to Margaret E. Kraft, who survives him. He settled in South Dakota in 1881 and has lived here ever since.

He leaves, besides his widow, a son, Elmer Gardner of Aberdeen, and a daughter, Mrs. Effie Fritz of Kansas City. He also has a sister, Mrs. Alice Markham of Rapid City, and a brother, Henry Gardner of Chetak, Wis.

Mr. Gardner was well known in this part of the state and was respected by all who knew him. He had held prominent positions in the city, being city weighmaster up to a few weeks ago.

The funeral will take place at 3 o'clock tomorrow afternoon at the Methodist church, and will be in charge of the G. A. R. The members of the G. A. R. and the W. R. C. will meet at the house at 2:30 and escort the remains to the be preached by Rev. J. W. Taylor. Interment will be in Riverside, and members of the G. A. R. will act as pall bearers.

Captain J. H. Hauser spoke the following at the funeral of
NELSON SLATER GARDNER:

"Enlisted in the Union Army in December, 1861, Co. A 19th Wisconsin Infantry. Until the following July the regiment acted as guard to Rebel prisoners when they were ordered to Norfolk, W. Va."

April, 1863 his Regiment was ordered to Suffolk and it was there he swam the Nansemond River. This Regiment saw service at Petersburg, was in the battle of Fair Oaks, where out of 190 men who went to battle only 44 came back. He was in Libby prison, Danville and Salisbury, NC

"At the battle of Fair Oaks in October, 1861 he received a wound to the head."

Discharged May 11, 1865

CAPTAIN J. H. HAUSER

I have not been able to verify the genealogy of the Gardner (Gardiner) family but believe the following to be accurate:

1. George Gardiner	b: about 1601 England
	d: 1673-76 Newport, RI
2. George	b: abt 1649 Newport
	d: 1724 N. Kingston, RI
3. Joseph	b: abt 1671 N.Kingston
	d: 1722 W.Greenwich

(not verified—also note died 8-22-26 Kingston)

4. George	b:1-4-1704 Narragansett, Washington, RI
	d.8-1-1801 Pownal, VT
Married Alice Browne	11-11-1737- W. Greenwich, KentRI
5. David	b: 1746 Newport
	d: 4-13-1813 Pownal
6. Solomon (Rev.)	b. 1790 Pownal
	d:6-7-59 E.Palerao,NY
Son of #4 Paul Gardner	b: 6-29—1743 W.Greenwich, Kent, RI
George	b: 6-3-79 W. Greenwich, Kent,RI
	d: 9-8-1839
Son: Oliver	b: 2-19-1767 Pownal, VT Bennington County
Wife: Olive Parker	married 12-18-87 (16 children)
Son: John	b: 11-15-1798 NY

         d: 12-20-1876
Wife: Polly Abby   married 1-23-1818
         b: 9-22-1799
         d: 6-4-1838
2nd Wife: Mary Ann Peso married 10-17-1838
         b: 1-4-1820
         d:1-25-1890
21 children born to John—Nelson Slater born to John and Mary Ann 1-1-1846 Elk Co., PA 2-22-03 info from Edward Gryczynski also Nicholson et al Family (Source: RootsWeb.com)

GARDNER GENEALOGY

CHILDREN	DOB	DOD	MARRIED
		1793 moved to Otsego, NY in 1823 to Clearfield, Elk Co, PA	
Oliver Gardner	2/19/1767	1841	
Married Olive	4-9-1770	8-21-1833	12-18-1787
Parker	10-4-1788	4-28-1817	Provided/Vidia Head? M before 1810
Phoebe	10-1789	10-26-1867	Charles Card-l-8-1806-had 10 children
Elsie (Eley)	6/10/1790	6-12-1881	Josoephus Potter M abt 1807 had 12-13 children
Judeah P.	12/2/1791	early 1852	Sally Jordan, Cowen married twice
Rath (Ruth):	3/4/1794	abt 1838	Elisha Weaver M abt 1812-1813
Sarah	8/17/1795		no more known
Benjamin	4/16/1797	after 1880	Mary/Polly George
John	11/15/1798	12/20/1876	see below
George W	12/3/1800	1883	Elizabeth Jordan M before 1829-3 sons died Civil War
Olive	7/18/1802	1855-1860	John Bedford George
Anna	6/4/1804		no more known
Polly	6/15/1805		no more known
Oliver, Jr.	2/16/1807	12-?-1874	Mary Litz dau of Rudoph m abt 1832
Elisha	12/7/1808	2-21-1890	Phoebe Jordan M 1-1-1828-13 children
Anna	6-30-1811		no more known
Charles R.	8/27/1812	1-18-1878	Nancy Litz dau of Rudolph M 10-4-1839
William M.	1818	3-6-1896	Mary DeForest M 1842 - 10 children

John	11/15/1798	12-20-1876	M 1-22-1818— 11 children
Polly Abby	9/22/1799	6/4/1838	
Mary Ann Peeso	1/4/1820	1/25/1890	M 10-17-1838 9 children
Shadrack	8/4/1819	11/27/1901	Phoebe Pearsall M abt 1844
Sally A	10/17/1820		no more is known
Phebe E.	12/6/1821		no more is known
Elsie P.	6/22/1822		no more is known
Judith P.	3/5/1825		no more is known
Olive W.	10/18/1826		she remained in Elk Co, PA when family moved W
Ann J.	5/16/1828		no more is known
Charolette	3/11/1830	Jun-02	Ben A. Cowen M 9-18-1847
Amasa M.	12/24/1831		no more is known 1850 census-living home
Erastus A	1/27/1834	12/20/1906	Janett Thompson M 2-18-1866
Bradford A.	5/7/1836	9-9-1864	Elizabeth McAllister M 2-8-1861 B. died Civil War
Jerome B.	11/16/1840	1866	Mary C. Hulbert Civil War disability
Sophronia'	4/25/1844	after 1910	Alexander McAllister- 1862 -John Johnson abt 1900
Nelson	1/1/1846	7/24/1909	Margaret Craft M 4-21-1866
Minerva	5/15/1849		no more is known
Jane	7-4-1854	4/18/1936	Arthur Knight abt 1872div 1880-Robert Martin 1891
Wallace	4-1856		Rachel Cunningham
Alice	9-1857	after 1910	Orrin Markham M abt 1876
Louisa-Lavis	abt 1861	9-16-1883	Orville Mitchell M 11-25-1877
Henry	1862-64?	after 1930	Lucy (?) Wynn M abt 1924

NELSON SLATER GARDNER

Nelson Slater Gardner was born January 1, 1846 In PA. He died July 24, 1909 in Aberdeen, SD

Nelson married Margaret Elizabeth Craft on April 21, 1866

Margaret was born December 16, 1848 and died August 1, 1933

Nelson and Margaret had a son, Charles, assumed died as an infant.

On May 16, 1867 Elmer Warren was born. He died October 12, 1949

Elmer married Ella Alemeda Dell in 1890, divorced and married Emma Crowley and that marriage ended in divorce also.

Daughter Effie Rebecca was born August 25, 1873 in Iowa and died 1967 in Chanute, Kansas. She married David R. Fritz on December 10, 1891. David was born in Mt Carroll, Ill. on May 9, 1864 and died November 23, 1944 in KS

David and Effie had four children. Ethel was born September 7, 1891 in Aberdeen, SD and died February 28, 1988 in OR

Elsie Christine born January 2, 1894 in Mt Carroll, ILL and died June 5, 1991in Sacramento, CA

The twins Mearl and Earl were born January 4, 1896 in Mt. Carroll, Ill and Earl Nelson died at the age of 100 on February 21, 1996. Mearl William died September 25, 1999. Both had resided in Phoenix, AZ and buried there.

Nelson Slater Gardner, Wife Margaret Daughter Effie, and son, Elmer
(Nelson & Margaret Craft married 4-23-1866)

Decendants of the CROFT family
One of the oldest families in Great Britian

JOHN HARTMAN CRAFT (changed in USA) anchestor from the Long Island Family

John born 1-1-1818 in Muncy Creek, Lacoming Co.,PA
   Died 3-18-1880 at Brainard, Fayette Co., Iowa

Married: 7-28-1842-Rebecca S. Peters
   Born 8-16-1822 Peterstown, VA
   Died 5-25-1905 Brainard, Iowa

Children:	
Henry Sovine	2-12-1845
Samual A.	11-6-1846
Margaret Elizabeth	12-16-1848
Mary Ann	4-27-1851
Sara (Sarah) Jane	4-27-1854
Jerusha Catherine	2-27-1856
John A.	2-9-1859
Clara Isabell	6-19-1861
Rebecca Luella	4-26-1862

Charles M. 11-16-1864

Amos 1872

Brainard was near the West line of Pleasant Valley and West Union, Iowa. John Craft (Margaret's father) gave the railroad free land across the 20 acre farm so track could be laid for a railroad. He worked in the brick yard located there.

Charles was owner of the only store and became depot agent.

Croft Castle

CROFT CASTLE

This ancient Castle on the Welsh border has existed since the 11th Century.

Sir Richard Croft fought at the battle of Mortimer's Cross nearby in 1461 and has a tomb in the church adjacent to the Castle.

In 1746 the 2nd Baronet disposed of the Castle to meet his debts to Richard Knight of the family of iron masters. The Croft family returned to the Castle again in 1923. The Castle passed from the 11th Baronet to 1st Lord Croft then to Major Owen Croft.

In 1956 the Castle came into the care of the National Trust and the furnishings all remain. The family retains the upper floor.

(My husband and I visited the Castle and spoke with the Honorable Diana in 1998. Hon. Nancy Diana Joyce Croft, Uhlman died November 28, 1999)

NELSON SLATER GARDNER

Nelson came home in August of 1865. The Civil War had come to a close. Over 600,000 lost their lives and almost 400,000 were wounded during this tragic war. At the time Nelson was captured 190 men went into action and 44 came back. His commanding officer, Lt. Colonel Strong, lost a leg at the time he was captured.

Nelson married his childhood sweetheart, Margaret Craft, in April 1866 at Brainard Station, Fayette County, Iowa.

In 1870 they were living with the Craft family in Pleasant Valley, Iowa. Their son, Elmer, was three years old.

In 1873 they were residing in Cresco, Iowa and their daughter, Effie, was born.

In 1880 the census states that Nelson was working as a teamster while they were living in Hutchinson, McLeod, MN (Effie then 7 and Elmer 13)

1880 The family moved to South Dakota in Ordway Township.

Civil War veterans were entitled to three rights under the Homestead Law in filing on government land. A homestead right, a pre-emption right and a tree claim right. Each right entitled the veteran to file on a quarter-section of land. In Ordway Township just northeast of Aberdeen, Nelson filed for his homestead. This was a distance of about 200 miles round trip to Watertown which was the nearest point to the homestead.

Ordway Township consisted of a general store, (the second story was later used for a time as the district school) harness business and later a Methodist church.

The "Gardner's" are noted as some of the earliest residents but Nelson Gardner and family were soon discouraged and the 1900 census shows them living in Aberdeen.

Nelson and Margaret established their home in Aberdeen. Nelson was noted as the City Weigh Master, Commander of the local G.A.R. and at the time of his death he was superintending a gang of men at the Culbert sand pit just out of town.

Nelson S. Gardner died July 24, 1909 having lived a full life. His widow Margaret, later married John Breidenbach and they continued to live in Aberdeen, S.D.

With the aid of computers we can locate statistics on our family members of long ago but what wonderful stories they could have told us that even modern technology can't give us. What a rare gift this diary from my great grandfather is to me and the family.

About the Author

I, and my husband of 64 years, were born in Kansas and spent our early years there. In 1955 we moved to Reno, Nevada and stayed in the area until ten years ago, when we moved to Mesa, Arizona, at what we call "our second retirement".

I worked many years in the insurance field and taught several adult classes for the University of NV Reno. I always liked to write stories but only for my own personal enjoyment. After moving to Arizona I joined a local writers group, and the interest continued.

At 82 years I wrote a coffee table book on my Mother's life and one on my husband for our son and daughter, grandchildren and the three great granddaughters. I've always been an avid reader and have loved history so it seemed only natural to write this book. I feel it leaves a heritage to the family of Nelson S. Gardner and gives you a personal insight about those that served in that Great War.

Author's Notes

Resources:

Dwinnell, S.A. material was collected from Reedsburg, WI, Free Press, Aug 9, 1872 and transcribed by John and Donna McCully, forwarded to me by Prof. Mike McCully. Also, C.A. Danforth articles, Jan 1926.

The following newspapers:
Prison Life article from the Baraboo Republic of Sauk Co, WI on May 30, 1895 — by W. O. Pietzsch
New York Tribune, Apr 19, 1855
Aberdeen Daily News, Sept 7, 1907

My editor, Dan Horne, for his expertise, time, and patience, many thanks.

Thank God for my answered prayers.

Effie Leatherman